The

Abell

Book of

Art

and

Verse

Sept. 23, 2019

COLLECTED BY TYLER ABELL

for Roy Meachum
with Warm Wishes,
Bess + Tyler Abell

Published July 2019
Printed in the USA

ISBN 978-0-578-52977-6

TABLE OF CONTENTS

George Abell was very proud
of his service in the U.S. Navy
during World War II.

George Abell and his grandson Dan in 1971
at George's birthday party.

George Abell, his son Tyler, and Azadia Newman
pose with a portrait of Tyler painted by Azadia.

INTRODUCTION

George Abell lived his life in rhyme
And you'd like to be his Valentine

His goal was to immerse in verse
The boors and rogues and politicians
Who railed about felonious ambitions

> Edited and arranged by Tyler Abell
> with apologies to his father

My father, George Abell, was a gifted poet, despite being a direct descendent (great-grandson) of a printer Arunah Shepherdson Abell – who founded the *Baltimore Sun* in 1837.

George Abell's first published poems that I can find appeared in the *Baltimore Sun* in 1923. I found one in the *New Yorker* magazine [June 15, 1929]. Although he never made a living with his poetry skill, many newspapers printed his verse, and the famous sportswriter Shirley Povich recalled having sonnet-writing contests with my father when they were both cub reporters for the *Washington Post*. Shirley moved on to sports writing for a small raise, I think $3.00 a week.

Though not all sonnets, George Abell poems appeared in the *Washington Star*, courtesy of columnist Betty Beale, and the *Times-Herald*, where he was promoted by its owner and his friend Eleanor "Cissy" Patterson. George Abell also wrote for the *Washington Daily News*, then after a stint in the Navy during World War II and with the occupation government in Germany, immediately after the war, he worked for *Time* and *Life* magazines in Paris and New York, then wound up his salaried career as Assistant Chief of Protocol – to Angie Duke, Lloyd Hand, James Symington, his son, and retired during the tenure of Emil "Bus" Mosbacher (circa 1970).

Remarkable artistry is displayed in the tiny (2" by 2 ½") paintings of fox, zebra, warthog, and deer. Painted by George Abell and used to decorate his home.

One of my fondest memories of my father was his artistic spontaneity. We frequently took in a movie on Friday afternoon (Friday was the day he had custody of me), and after the movie, we stopped at Brentano's bookstore on F Street near the theatre. On the way to his apartment in Georgetown, he sat in the cab (he never did drive) and composed a dedication in verse inside the book he had just purchased for me, and sometimes with a cartoon sketch. All in ink and no scratch overs during a short cab ride. Unfortunately, I've been separated from those books. A few examples he did in the 1970s have survived, including *The Kentucky Derby* and Lord Nelson's biography. But why should I continue to write about the poems when the best way to enjoy them is to read them, which my father did. Reciting his poems out loud was a favorite way to amuse his family and friends.

He also had Brian Brown illustrate *The Hippo with Political Aspirations* and paint parts of that poem on the walls of the bathroom in his Georgetown apartment.

READ ON

How Poems Are Arranged and Why

Spontaneity was a thread running through George Abell's verse, and it frequently connected with current events, but just as often it did not. I have elected to use categories, which at some unknown time he chose. And I underscore <u>unknown time</u> because although he worked in the U.S. Office of Protocol from about 1962 to 1970, his writings reflect an interest in protocol and politics throughout his life.

Some poems appeared in two categories, so I narrowed the use to what I felt was the most appropriate category.

TRAVELS IN PROTOCOL

A LONDON SHOWER

With utter and complete disdain
Lord Abernethy viewed the rain,
Holding his new umbrella furled
As if to taunt the drizzly world.
"I shall not," Abernethy said,
"Unfurl it by a single thread."
Then, blithely as a springtime flower,
He tripped into the teeming shower.

The downpour swept in sullen sheets
Across the flooded London streets.
It gurgled grimly in the gutters;
It dripped from roofs and window shutters,
It splashed from Abernethy's hat
And trickled down his wet cravat –
An Ascot (for, as was the case,
He'd planned to see the Ascot race).

Yet, quite undaunted, debonair,
Lord Abernethy sniffed the air
And gazed upon the tiny town.
He vowed "This will not get me down"
And through a puddle gaily stepped
O'er which two girls with poodles leapt.
The poodles slipped. One drowned. The other
Would soon have perished like his brother,
But Abernethy with a shout
(And his umbrella!) fished him out.
"Quite possibly it had a cramp,"
Said he. "Today is rather damp.
I'm sure," he added, "That this shower
Will end at least within the hour."

It ended later than he thought.
Lord Abernethy quickly caught

A cold. Pneumonia set in.
He met it with uplifted chin.
Like Cyrano de Bergerac
His Brigg umbrella from the rack
He took and, waving it with pride,
"God Save the Queen!" he cried – and died.

BUYING ELK-SKIN GLOVES IN NORWAY

The salesman sadly shook his head:
"We have no elk-skin gloves," he said.
"We have fine gloves of Arctic fox,
Of water buffalo and ox,
Of reindeer, possum, mink and mole,
Of cat's fur and Siberian sole."
He paused – he seemed about to cry,
"I want some elk-skin gloves," said I.

"We have," the salesman hurried on,
"Unlathered sheep gloves from Ceylon,
Unbleached gloves of Alaskan seal,
Unblemished gloves of virgin veal,
Gloves undeclared from Timbuctoo,
Unspeakable, unused, non-U"—
I cut into his wild tirade,
"I want some elk-skin gloves," I said.

"Would you," the salesman tried again,
"Settle for gloves of cellophane,
Or Persian lamb or fractured silk,
Or nylon dipped in buttermilk?"
I brought his ravings to an end.
"I want some elk-skin gloves, my friend."
The salesman sadly shook his head.
"We're out of elk-skin gloves," he said.*

*n.b. But I was able to buy some, nonetheless!

COCKTAILS AT SCHIAPARELLI'S

It was Paris! It was London! It had something of New York!
It was caviar and rubies on an old Picasso fork.
It was phonies! It was fairies! It was veddy, veddy nice!
It was Matisse and baloney – cut me another slice!
It was diamonds on a stuffed shirt! It was oxtail in the belly!
My dear, it was "tout-Paris" meeting Elsa Schiaparelli!

You walked across the zebra skins down to a formal garden
Where a whiff of dead mimosa cut the stink of Lizzie Arden.
Schiap in an old potato-sack of sky-blue crepe de chine,
Stood elegantly greeting each arriving social queen.
As one snaked a careful passage toward the champagne and the scotch,
One nervously held onto both one's wallet and one's watch,
For in all that gay assemblage there was scarcely one in nine,
But would blithely sell you profits in a nonexistent mine.

There was someone from the Travellers Club, a desiccated wreck
With a celluloid collar round his scrawny, bird-like neck;
There was someone of the Scranton News and whoosit of the Times;
There was someone jingling bracelets with a lot of golden chimes;
There was faded Lady something wearing gloves of faded rose,
And piloting a youthful niece among her faded beaux.
There was chubby Mrs. What's-her-name with diamonds on her arms
Exuding in flamboyant grace her rare exotic charm.

Like a vision of Nokomis in her yellow nightmare hat,
One noted – oh, I don't know who – engaged in pleasant chat.
But if the pleasure mutual was, her listener did not say,
She clutched him with a skinny claw each time he edged away.
There were funny, creaky generals out of Siam and Peru;
There were scruffy, stodgy persons out of Bradstreet and Who's Who;
There were most amusing creatures gulping whiskey by the pail,
If they were out of anywhere, it must have been a jail!

There were dames like ancient mariners with fierce and glittering eyes
Who held with malicious leer the men that sidled by;

There was one who looked exactly like an inimitable Zerbe;

There was something with a bosom whom his friends all hailed as "Herbie";

There were melancholy ladies with a melancholy air

Who seemed ever sadly looking for someone who wasn't there;

There were also, with a flower and a swish of protocol,

An exquisite little zero with an antiquated doll.

It was Paris! It was Rio! And a tiny breath of Rome!

It was even the Riviera... But it surely wasn't home!

It was turtle soup at sunset! It was pansies! It was punks!

It was gorgeous old chinchilla taken out of horse-hair trunks!

It was mothballs creased in aspic! It was jewels in the jelly!

My dear, it was "tout-Paris" meeting Elsa Schiaparelli!

COOK VERSUS FRENCH CHEF

A cook should be fat as an old Dutch queen
And even a little bit sweaty
From bending over a hot tureen
And sniffing sprouts and spaghetti.

A good French chef, on the other hand,
Should always be thin and quiet,
And twist his moustache and look very grand
When anyone speaks of a diet.

If the soup is burned the cook should snap:
"Well, hell, that's the way soups are!"
But the chef should calmly remove his cap
And drown in the "Bisque a l'Homard!"

IBO BEACH BY MOONLIGHT

There are no drums except the waves that pound
In fretful cadence on the moon-blanched shore,
Yet from the walls of conscience comes a sound
Like breathing heard beyond a half closed door.

Listen! There is but sea and soughing wind.
Look! There is only beauty, depth and light.
Why then this sadness which one feels behind
The flashing silver armor of the night?

DINER MACABRE

I'm dining tonight with a dead Maharanee
Tawny as tigers that crouch in the night
With elegant shoulders like elephant boulders
That shiver and quiver whenever she's tight.

Glitteringly cold is the gem in her nostril,
Flaky with gold are the teeth in her head,
Biting, inviting, one's sense delighting –
She's really exciting – except that she's dead!

How to describe her – that dead Maharanee?
Picture a dream queen of ex-King Farouk's
Quite hippopotamy, rather more bottomy
Than one expects of respectable spooks!

I'm dining tonight with my dead Maharanee,
Unless _you_ will dine, dear, at half after eight.
If you no kind do, I'll dine my Hindu,
My ectoplasmic East Indian date.

DINING "AL FRESCO" IN ITALY

Beneath the vine Italians dine
Deliriously "al fresco."
Such is, they say, the surest way
To romance... Well, I guess so!

Although I'd rather kiss some miss
Who'd never seen a spider
Than sleep with one who has at least
A score or so inside her!

Honeymoon Hysteria

They thought that love came straight from above,
But the gods were maybe nappin'
When they sailed in June on their honeymoon
And strange things started to happen.

He wanted to go to a place that's hot –
No matter what it costed –
Where the wild baboon stays in bed till noon,
(The heat gets it so exhausted.)

Where the girls don't wear anything but hair –
Not even a brief bikini –
And a piece of ice costs a hell of a price
To dip in a warm martini.

She wanted to go to a place that's cold,
Where Santa Claus is a hero,
And the polar bears all sweat in their lairs
When the temperature goes above zero,

Where and icicle forms on the postman's toe
Instead of the usual callous,
And the hottest show in town is the glow
Of Aurora Borealis.

It's easy to see they couldn't agree –
The thing was really uncanny
She wanted frost on her morning toast
He wanted frangipani.

She SHE rushed back home and HE stayed in Rome,
And they glared across the Atlantic,
And HE found a gal who's his "pizza pal" –
And SHE – well, she's simply frantic!

How To Be a Perfect Guest

(Notes at Marjorie Merriweather Post's Camp Topridge in the Adirondacks)

I'm a terrible guest –
Can't stand "hikes,"
Distrust tricycles,
Won't ride bikes.
Loathe picnics
(Bugs in the food!)
What about badminton?
Not in the mood.
We're planning a "portage"...
Plan it alone!
Phoning all house guests...
Not on <u>my</u> phone!
Sure, I'm impossible!
What do I wish?
Just to laze around,
Loaf, read, fish,
Write if I feel like it –
Drink if I don't.
Ask a girl will she dance,
Hope that she won't.
Breakfast in bed,
Coffee that's hot –
Come to the breakfast room?
Certainly not!
Call me a bore, a ham,
A poor sport, a pest –
Just call me what I am –
A wonderful guest!

Muddled Mallorca Soliloquy (After Three Martinis)

O Island of the pig and peach –
(Or is it goat and cheese?) I reach
Nostalgic arms to cuddle each
Lean porker!

I rate thee higher far than Sark,
Than Corsica – all grim and stark –
Than Cyprus or – let me remark –
Minorca!

All hail to groves of luscious lime –
To bells that clang and never chime –
To trains that never run on time –
Mallorca!

I love – as Chopin loved George Sand –
Thy mountains, purple, proud and grand,
Thy gambas faintly spiced with sand
Mallorca!

I like thy priests so sleek and fine
O Island of the peach and pine.
(Or is it antelope and wine?)
Mallorca!

I love thy women spinning flax –
In picturesque paisano hats,
Surrounded by their many cats,
Mallorca!

I love thy harbors wherein rub
Bright-painted sloop and battered tub,
Old Lima tramp and Snorker sub –
(Or is it Snorker?)

I much admire each patient plow,
Land of the apricot and cow.

(Or is it cantaloupe and sow?)
Mallorca!

I love thy olives – fairly well –
I love thy ensaimada smell –
I love – I love – Oh what the hell –
Mallorca!

MUSINGS OF KING FERDINAND, 1492

Spain and a glorious morning – the twenty-first of July.

Not one Moor in Granada! Not one cloud in the sky!

Reminds me of Spring in Huesca – Those foreigners drank too much!

Juan of Flanders goes berserk – What's to expect from the Dutch?

I'm sick of these Flemish painters. Oh, I admit they can paint,

But, after all, pigments are costly and they all lack our self-restraint.

Santos with silver halos, angels with harps of gold –

Why can't they do me a landscape, dignified, dark and cold?

I dream sometimes of our mountains – Moncayo, heavy with snow –

And the stretches of our Maestrazio with its somber, beguiling glow,

They talk here of fruit and bonbons (Isabella's getting too fat!)

And rave over figs and olives – What do they know about that?

Give me our native olives, mulberries, almonds, wine!

Our violent storms in the summer! Our forests of beech and pine!

We Aragonese may be stubborn – we hammer nails with our heads –

But we work and we're calm as oxen and don't sleep in others' beds!

Imagination? Who needs it?... Humph! Isabella, of course,

Surrounded by pimps and artists! I prefer, Paco, my horse.

He doesn't fiddle with brushes or primp like a lady's hound,

Or plot out routes to the Indies, or think that the world is round.

What is the name of her latest? Isn't he Genovese?

Cristobal something-or-other – always falls at her knees

And begs for a private audience – nothing unlawful. I mean

How can a king be jealous, especially over his Queen?

Once down in Tarazona – let's forget about her.

My Father-Confessor said Masses and read the Confiteor

For months from the public pulpit, he really gave me a fright.

My fingers grew calloused as anvils, telling my beads in the night.

Now, I govern three Kingdoms – call it four with Castile.

I've conquered the heights of Granada and brought the Arabs to heel.

Here in this Muslim throne room, I hold a Christian court.

A man would term it "ambition," Isabella treats it as sport.

Dressmakers, dwarfs and tumblers ...painters and poets galore –

Foreigners! Madre de Dios! And then the Genovese bore!
Garrulous? God, what a talker! Unrolling map and chart,
Pointing, explaining, shrugging, placing his hand on his heart.
Florentine, Roman, Venetian! One could but guess his state.
I merely found him tiresome but others said he was great,
Great as an ocean Admiral wearing a sailor's hat –
(How could a brilliant seaman deny that the world is flat?)
Ah, I recall his name now! A person of lowly birth...
Cristoforo Columbus, the biggest fool on this earth!

No Names, Please!

I wooed her by the sea at Mantoloking;
I sought her as an insect seeks the flame.
But somehow – and this really is provoking –
I never can recall the woman's name.

I know her eyes were like exotic saucers,
Her breasts were like a starlet's bid to fame.
But though her lines were better far than Chaucer's,
I can't recall the wretched creature's name.

She kissed me after swigging a Manhattan.
She introduced me to her kin and kith.
Her name was... let me see... Was it Mountbatten?
No, no, now!... I remember – it was Smith!

Some day perhaps we'll meet in Rome or Paris
And talk in well-bred, over-cultured tones,
And maybe I will call her Mrs. Harris.
I hope that she will call <u>me</u> Mr. Jones!

ON PLEASING A LADY

He made no plans because plans can be changed
And his personal program he knew.
He didn't know, though, that he thus disarranged
The things <u>she</u> decided to do.

They journeyed by steamer, by car and by plane
Over ocean and valley and dale.
<u>She</u> was impatient and made it quite plain
<u>She</u>'d wanted to travel by rail.

He knew the bliss of an old Bordeaux wine,
A place where the connoisseurs stop –
He didn't know <u>she</u>'d determined to dine
At a restaurant next to a shop.

He chose an inn unobtrusively neat
Conveniently close to the Strand,
<u>She</u> said the Aubussons gave her sore feet
And wished they had stayed at the Grand.

He yearned for caviar, <u>she</u> sighed for hock.
He was for icy champagne,
<u>She</u> believed Bourbon was better than Bach,
And fish eggs were bad for the brain.

<u>She</u> wanted service and rooms with a view
He wanted old tawny port.
He did things <u>she</u> expected him to
And ended in bankruptcy court.

On Seeing a Titled, Turbaned Passenger Aboard Ship

I don't know where he's from
Or if he's smart or dumb
Or even why he's come
To the States.
He's silent as a sphynx,
So I can't guess what he thinks
Or what he eats and drinks,
Whom he dates.

Do you suppose at home
He is like the Pope in Rome?
Does his palace have a dome?
Or a moat?
Do the people he controls
Follow socialistic goals
Or merely follow polls?
Do they vote?

Are his jungles full of smells
And exciting whoops and yells?
Do his wives wear tinkling bells
'Round their necks?
Are the local habits quaint?
Do the women use restraint
Or do they swoon and faint
Over sex?

He may be just a clown
Or he may have great renown
And wear emeralds in his crown
Big as limes;
But whatever he may be
Or do, he is to me
An entrancing parody
Of our times.

On the Frenzy of Mountain Climbing

(A Tyrolean Thought)

I think that I could gladly scalp
A man who raves about an Alp –
The Weldenstern, the Bammerglitz,
The Oberpfaffen, Glamorspitz,
The Rottenhorn, the Gross Bestude,
The Salzflurr, or the Unterglude.

My friend, my earnest friend, forbear!
You've climbed them – well, what do I care?
But tell me, have you never yet
Heard of Der Grosser Alphabet?...
Then do not waste my precious time
Ranting of crags like Wetterheim
Or Zugenkratz or Berzufall
Or... God knows what... I've climbed them all.
Ach, shones Tag! Before we met
I climbed Der Grosser Alphabet!

O Liederkranz! O Bel Paese!
That crazy mountain drives me crazy!
It seems my very soul to smother!
It calls me like a long-lost brother!
It makes me dream of Hans und Fritzel!
It haunts me like a Wiener Schnitzel!......
Which is precisely why next week
I must return to scale that peak –
O Wunderbar! O Apfel Strudel!......
Who claims it once has lost his noodle......
Who climbs it twice must ever yet
Conquer Der Grosser Alphabet!

PAPERS IN PARIS

Upon my desk the papers lie,
Tier upon tier, serene and high,
It does me good to see them there...
LE FIGARO, LE POPULAIRE,
THE HERALD-TRIB, L'HUMANITE,
THE NEW YORK TIMES, LA LIBERTE,
L'AURORE, FRANCE-SOIR, LA TABLE RONDE,
LA CROIX, THE DAILY MAIL, LE MONDE...
What world news can a writer miss
Who is so well informed as this?

I gather up with greatest care
LE FIGARO, LE POPULAIRE,
THE HERALD-TRIB, L'HUMANITE,
THE NEW YORK TIMES, LA LIBERTE,
L'AURORE, FRANCE-SOIR, LA TABLE RONDE,
LA CROIX, THE DAILY MAIL, LE MONDE...
I add the PARIS-PRESSE and MATCH,
And carry home the biggest batch
Of papers published under the sun.
I never read a God-damned one!

PICKPOCKET IN GRANADA

How curious is people's pride!
One boasts to be a tourist guide,
Another fights in bull-ring with espada,
One cares to dive for pearls in sea
Or likes to dig the earth. <u>Not</u> <u>me</u>!
I pick the passing pocket in Granada.

Mostly fortunately my mother's niece
Is with the captain of police
For very many happy years "cassada,"
Which is the reason why his men
Don't throw me into prison when
I pick the passing pocket in Granada.

Americans are rich, they say.
They fight for gold, they bribe, they pay
To get themselves divorces in Nevada.
But, tell me, whose is greater sin –
His who schemes much gold to win,
Or his who picks the pocket in Granada?

THE MARGATE ELEPHANT

In the summer of 1882
A man who had nothing better to do
Hating his neighbors, bored with his wife,
Evolved the great idea of his life.

Maybe the stunt had a business pitch
Or perhaps he was just a mean S.O.B.
Or else his mind had begun to skid –
Anyhow, here is what he did.

He built an elephant four stories high –
Little round windows in place of each eye,
A kind of a house with closets and stairs
And toilet (now in need of repairs).

He painted his elephant dirty grey
And looked at the thing and said "Take it away!"
But no one could take it and there it stands
Solid and sad on the Margate sands.

Facing the ocean with blank, dull look
Like something out of jungle book
Written for giants in bygone times
And illustrated with giant rhymes.

Plaster is peeling off of its tusks
And its once bright howdah is mostly husks
Of tin and tinsel. For 50 cents
(A quarter for children) you cross a fence

And climb right up the elephant's rear
And inside its stomach and past its ear
In fact, you can just go anywhere –
What does the poor old elephant care?

Serene, impassive, the creature stands
Gazing over the Margate sands
Alone, unaffected, as if it thought
All the excitement about it naught,

Beneath it children romp and shout
And hot dog stands are scattered about
Hordes of tourists in paper caps
With messy babies clutched in their laps,

Jostling and yelling, pause to gape
At the elephant's huge unwieldy shape.
A sign says "OPEN" so up they go
To yell some more at the crowds below.

Up they go to the very top –
Brother and sister and Mom and Pop,
Uncle and cousin and grandma too,
Climbing to see the lovely view.

Screaming, pointing, smearing gum
Over the gray cracked walls where some
Would-be artists and litterateurs
Have scribbled and scrawled some fancy blurs.

Removed from all this wild commotion,
The elephant gazes over the ocean
Imperturbable, peeling, quaint,
A monstrous relic of self-restraint.

If it could speak, its words might be
A bit disconcerting to you and me –
For it might say (it could go so far!)
"What God damn fools all you humans are!"

THE PHAROAH OF THE FAIR

You'll hear his name in whispers on the Pepsi-Cola ride
Or find it faintly scribbled where the Glider gliders glide,
But only when the Sky Ride lifts you safely in the air,
Must you speak aloud of Moses – King and Pharoah of the Fair!

He wears no golden cobra on his softly sweating dome,
No Africans with peacock fans escort his chariot home.
Nor do the shades of Isis and Anubis with a smile
Observe his barge's gleaming prow divide with sacred Nile.

His cobra is a serpent tongue to vilify the press,
His retinue a slave or two recruited by duress.
His pyramids are built of bids by each concessionaire
To glorify His Majesty, the Pharoah of the Fair!

No sandals of Obsidian enshrine his sockless feet,
He crushes opposition with a shoe from Fulton Street.
No tasseled troops from Nubia attack the honky-tonks,
The girlie-girlie shows succumb to hoodlums from the Bronx.

And, tho' in ancient Egypt they'd have locked him in a vault,
Poletti thinks spaghetti will atone for any fault.
Our modern pharaoh feels he'll know what's good enough for plebes,
To hell with what they used to do in antiquated Thebes.

Why should he hearken to advice? A Pharoah bows to none,
Do not his edicts and decrees proclaim: "My will be done!
Let those of you who wish to view The Fair fork out that tax!
Let those who criticize my reign beware the headman's axe!"

"Let Ford protest and beat his breast! Let General Motors stew!
Let Spain in pain demand in vain a great revenue!
Let Disney fret and Bell regret its telephonic splurge!
If Gas and G.E. lose their shirt – God damn it, let them merge!"

Editor's Note: George Abell spelled "Pharoah" like the
2015 Triple Crown winner several decades early.

Thus spake the Chief and small relief falls from his lifeless lips,
Nor does he try to tell you why The Fair is in eclipse.
So, on your knees, ye Pharisees, and say a little prayer.
"For Moses?" do I hear you ask? "No dumbbells!! For The Fair!"

WHEN IN ROME

Said Appius Claudius to his son:
"In Rome hard drinking isn't done."
Said Appius, Jr.: "Still I think
That I am Appius when I – hic! – drink!"

WHY, OH WHY?

Pray tell me, Lady Chatterjee,
Why did you not embark?
Although we were to sail at three,
They held the ship 'till dark.

What vagrant whim or mania
Possessed you, dear, to stop
The R.M.S. "Sylvania"
From her Atlantic hop?

The Captain waited on the bridge,
The stewards down below.
We place your orchids in the fridge,
Then – well, we had to go!

O absent Lady Chatterjee,
Your name was on the list,
And were you Lady Chatterley
You couldn't be more missed!

And though your memory from afar
Grow nebulous and pale,
I'll always wonder who you are
And why you did not sail!

ANIMAL CRACKERS

A Childish Error

When Alexander crept downstairs
He thought that two new teddy bears
Were added to his nursery.
But grizzly bears on children sup,
They gobbled Alexander up
In manner quick and cursory.

Circumstantial Evidence

When Harry shot and later put his little dog on ice,
The Judge declaimed in fiery monologue
But Harry kept repeating and ignored the court's advice:
"The jam was on the whiskers of the dog!"

"I found the jam-pot empty when I staggered down the stairs
To pour myself the nightly shot of grog –
And what did I discover when I raised the lap dog's ears?
The jam was on the whiskers of the dog!"

"It could have been Amanda Lou, a truly greedy slut –
It could have been my baby's golliwog –
It could have been a passing tramp by hunger driven, but
The jam was on the whiskers of the dog!"

The judge declared: "You are the kind of person I delight
To send to jail and frequently to flog."
Still Harry stubbornly replied: "Your Honor may be right,
But the jam was on the whiskers of the dog."

A Mosquito's Advice to His Son

Good Father Mosquito felt swell
His Doctor had given him hell
But he stole furtive bites
On malarial nights
And swigs from an old stagnant well.

He buzzed at his droopy young son:
"See here! You are now 21 —
And 21 days in a number of ways,
Should teach you the meaning of fun!"

"We are lodged in a very fine house
Our hostess, you know, is a souse.
And her friends, and the maid—How's that? You're afraid?
Say! —Are you Mosquito or Mouse?"

"The strategy's simple and short
"She's had a full bottle of port.
"She's drunk—just your dish
"What more do you wish?
"A smart presentation at Court?"

"Be cagey—don't linger—don't shirk
"Don't try any fanciful quirk—
"But hum all you want
"It's your family's vaunt
"That music goes well with our work!"

"Remember your background, my boy!
"Your granddad bit Admiral McCloy.
"You need blood and meat
"Before sinking a fleet
"Zip along! Zip away! Zip ahoy!"

Mosquito Mansion
26 Ave. Victor Hugo
Paris, August 1951

ECLIPSE OF THE BADGER

In Devonshire a badger lived,
Respected, honored, praised and smug,
Because the bristles on his chest
Were longer than a woman's tongue.

More famed was he than China tea
Or even English marmalade;
His itchy, scratchy bristles made
Him master of the export trade.

"Buy British Badger!" was the cry
That echoed from a thousand lips,
And badger bristles packed in brine
Held down the hulls of British ships.

"Wee British Badger" was a brush
Designed by Saks and Lizzy Arden;
"Hail, British Badger" was the play
That made a hit at Covent Garden.

"Best British Badger" was the sign
That flashed in fire on Piccadilly;
While "Dear Old Badger" was a song
For college kids – and awfully silly.

One never saw a swifter rise
On stock exchange recorded yet.
The badger's mother went and bought
A TV-wireless-deep-freeze set.

Where once his father used to ride
In modest pride a double-decker,
A Bentley brought him every week
To squeak at lords of the Exchequer.

Although at heart he steadfast stayed
A simple creature without frills,
Sir Briton Badger breakfasted
On caviar and dollar bills.

"Buy British Badger!"... But the cry
Ascended to a wailing scream
When, puncturing the badger's dream,
Appeared a <u>brushless</u> shaving cream!

In vain the badger family tried
To buy up shares from brother gophers.
They could not stem the brushless tide
Which even swept out horsehair sofas!

Electric razor zoomed like mad
And ruined badger bristles shippers;
Sir Briton Badger (horrors!) had
To breakfast now on tea and kippers.

There came a morning when – no joke –
One kipper gleamed upon the shelf.
Poor Mother Badger had a stroke
And Father Badger shot himself.

So if some day along the road
Poor Briton Badger you should see,
Don't be surprised if he should frown
And growl at you "Don't badger me!"

GENEROUS PAPA

An aged hunter who had come
To India for his liver,
Strolled with his little girl beside
A hippo-spotted river.

"The hippopotamus, my child,
Is quite a bully creature.
The animal has not, we're told
A single wooly feature."

"It sings a song of dreamy love
Unto its mate for hours.
It roams unhampered through the park
And feeds on fish and flowers."

"Come, come, my child... don't be afraid!"
He led her to the water
And caught a hippo by its tail
And gave it to his daughter.

IRISH DOGS

I love the damp, soft-footed dogs
That creep through fields at dawn –
Not pugs that lie like lifeless logs
Upon a sun-baked lawn.

I scorn your pampered Pekingese,
Your poodles primped and rare
Give me the Irish dogs with fleas
And raindrops in their hair.

HABEAS DOGUS

The case seemed clear. In canine court
The plaintiff, Rev. Poodle Jones,
A most important suit had brought
For damages – ten thousand bones.

Jones charged that on October one
He'd found, after a three-day search,
The son-of-a-bitch who'd peed upon
A pillar of the Baptist Church.

"And there he stands." Jones waved a paw
Dramatically at Boxer Brown.
"Your Honor, sir, I claim the law
Against the dirtiest dog in town."

"He has no morals, he's a cur.
He raped a little Chow last Spring.
Despite my sacred calling, sir,
I'd like to see this scoundrel swing."

"Thump!" went the gavel. "Thump" once more.
Old Justice Schnauzer glowered down
And bent upon the reverend bore
His stern if somewhat weary frown.

"No names!" Judge Schnauzer barked. "Just fact!
I'll have you for contempt of court.
You state opinions quite unbacked
By any rationale of thought."

"Good sons-of-bitches are we all
And dogs are dirty now and then,
But 'scoundrel' is a term like 'pal'--
Both used exclusively by men."

"And rape with us is not a crime.
A peccadillo, sir, at most.
As for your pillar of the church,
Perhaps he took it for a post."

"But, Judge," whined Rev. Poodle Jones,
"This pillar of the church – that's me.
He leaked on me! Ten thousand bones
Can scarce restore my dignity."

Judge Schnauzer's wrinkled face grew bleak,
As autumn hills are chilled by frosts.
"Defendant guilty of a leak!
One T-bone steak, well done, with costs!"

JAP RAT-EATER OR RAT JAP-EATER?

"TOKYO, August 30 (UP)— Ichiro Akimoto, 59, told the newspaper
Mainichi today that he would offer free room and board to any woman
who was willing to marry him and didn't mind the fact that he eats 24 rats
a month. Akimoto, who said rats 'taste just like chicken' disclosed that he
had acquired the taste during the war."

In wartime days in old Japan
Times plenty hard for average man.
When Akimoto want to eat
He peek in stove and see no meat.
He sharpen knife; he look around.
He figure something must be found.
He hear a queak; he hear a swish.
"Aha," he snicker. "Rats my dish."
With knife plus brains and bamboo stick,
He kill one hundred rats real quick.
"Banzai," he gloat. "Can doing nice
With such-like beasts or even mice."
Soon, Akimoto growing fat,
Tasting each day delicious rat.

But wartime end in old Japan.
Times still quite hard for average man.
Now, Akimoto sheathe his knife.

He tell around he wish a wife.
And more. He seek a woman who
Think rats first-rate in daily stew.
No doing. Lose face. Wives crave bees
Or birds. No rats. So sorry, please!
Then, Akimoto go to press
To advertise his great distress.
"Wife get free lodging. Rats no bite.
Taste just like chicken," so he write.

Is certain sure, he inform friend,
That girls respond and problem end.

Yet, who can tell? Who reconstrue
What Jap who eat the rat may do?
In old Japan, one thing they say,
But doing quite the other way.
Suppose, when Akimoto's wife
Arrive, he take his butcher knife
And question: "Sweetheart, how by you?
Life good, death better. Is not true?"
Then, wife inquire: "Pray tell me why
You speak so feelingly to die?
Pray why rats sit at table here
With happy grin from ear to ear?"
Then Akimoto make a bow:
"So sorry. They my house-guests now."

ON SEEING THE DOG HOUSE OF MARIE ANTOINETTE'S PET TERRIER AT VERSAILLES

I wonder what they thought
In that faded, jaded court
When the Queen
Acquired a dog that lay
In a dog house by Boucher
Gold and green?

Did the Princesse de Lamballe
Gasp "Quel charmant animal!"
Did the King
In his blunt, good-humored way
Belch delightedly and say:
"Just the thing!"

Did the Duc de Richelieu
Roll his eyes and sigh: "Mon Dieu!
Bigger debts!"
Did the courtiers, taking snuff,
Sneer: "Her lovers aren't enough.
She needs pets."

Did His Majesty grow red
When the dog peed on the bed
Of his wife,
And refuse it sips of wine
And partridge sliced up fine
With a knife?

When the dreadful days dame on
And the rose of Trianon
Ceased to bloom,
Did the little dog die too?
Did they beat it black and blue
With a broom?

I <u>sort of</u> like to think
That it didn't cringe or slink,
Whine or beg,
But that it made a pass
At Robespierre's bony ass
Or his leg!

ON SENDING A STEUBEN GLASS EAGLE
TO THE CROWN PRINCE OF LIECHTENSTEIN

The regal eagle spread its pinions
Across imperial Rome's dominions
And Austrian emperors long since dead
Gave it an extra Hapsbourg head.

But now its Steuben head will shine
On the dull cows in Liechtenstein
And spread Napoleonic views
Among the peasants of Vaduz.

ON THE DANGER OF HEART ATTACKS

An ancient lobster swimming in the sea
Heard music playing from a seaside quay
"What is that tune?" he asked in some amaze.
A passing fish replied: "The Marseillaise."
"The mayonnaise!" he echoed, horrified,
And choked and had a heart attack and died.

ON THE DEATH OF A PET DOG

In halcyon days along remembered paths
He raced beside me, knowing only life,
Cherishing nothing in his clouded mind
Except thin dreams of summer, food, manure;

Perhaps the smell of bitches, urine dried
On a chopped stump by some Norwegian fjord,
The sting of dust in Provence where an inn
Offered well-water to assuage his thirst.

Such things belong to dogs, and doglike, cling
To memory, chocking back the fancied scene:
The brave Llewellyn flecked with lupine blood –
The noble Brutus grieving by the hearth.

So Topolino lived, yet not less mourned
Than Brutus or Llewellyn, sweet with Christ;
Spared – pagan that he was – our Christian pomps
And all our idiot panoply of death.

OPERATIC KITTY

A cat perched on a cellar door
Trilled "Lucia di Lammermoor"
In horrible falsetto;
But one young guy returning soused
From an affair where he's caroused,
Cried: "Sing the 'Jewel Song' from 'Faust'!"
And flung out a libretto.

On the Senseless Starting of Arguments

A tiger in a barroom sat
And quietly imbibed his drinks.
The Barman, amiable and fat,
Behind his bar caught forty winks.

Then suddenly a clock struck eight.
The Barman opened sleepy eyes,
And, swallowing a whiskey straight,
Gazed at the Tiger in surprise.

"Your face," said he, "upon my life,
Reminds me of a cat I met
Long years ago. He killed my wife
When we were hunting in Tibet!"

The Tiger placidly replied:
"My family from India came.
So, if some stranger killed your bride,
I scarcely can assume the blame."

"Your nose," the Barman said, "forsooth,
Betrays a vaguely ursine air.
Do you suppose that in his youth
Your father wooed a female bear?"

"My father's loves," the Tiger said,
"Are hardly pertinent tonight.
For many years he has been dead.
Pray, do you wish to start a fight?"

"A fight! Why no!" the other sneered.
"In peace then let me sip my beer" –
"Or human blood," the Barman jeered.
"We do not trust your species here!"

The Tiger yawned and with a frown
Arose, superb the tense grim,
Gulped half a quart of Bourbon down –
Then tore the Barman limb from limb!

PROTOCOL IN THE JUNGLE

The Lion convened a great council of State
And called on the principal regents
To explain for their good how each animal stood,
According to rules of precedence.

The Fox cried: "I'm first. I have cunning and wit.
No other my gifts can inherit."
But the Wolf and the Bear and the soft-footed Hare
Each claimed a particular merit.

All skulking devices the Elephant scorned,
And spoke of his brain as "terrific,"
Though the Jaguar jeered and the Antelope sneered:
"It's large – if you're being specific."

The jungle went wild as the bickering beasts
Endeavored their rights to deteremine.
And with claw, tooth and tusk they debated 'till dusk
When the Lion arose in his ermine.

"I am King," he declared as he tilted his crown
Rather rakishly over his eyebrows.
"I am first on the list, for I always insist
Precedence belongs to the high-brows."

"After me come the ranks of the eaters of flesh––
The Tigers, the Panthers, the Leopards––
Then the armored elite, then the sheep which we eat
When they're badly protected by shepherds.

"You have argued and quarreled and quibbled in vain,
And all that I find is a bungle.
This protocol nonsense just gives me a pain.
<u>TO EAT IS THE LAW OF THE JUNGLE!</u>"

SEA-GULL SOLILOQUY IN DENMARK

As I sip my chocolate maltic
Looking out upon the Baltic,
I remember what my grandpapa averred:
"Other birds take time for chewing
But the gull knows what he's doing,
For the sea-gull is an independent bird!"

So I watch the sea-gulls gleaming,
Circling, swooping, always screaming...
(They really are a little bit absurd!)
And yet one must admire them.
Even screaming doesn't tire 'em
For the sea-gull is an independent bird.

With a sweeping, graceful motion
They grab garbage from the ocean –
The floating stuff at which the fish demurred.
They'll eat caviar or copper.
Hell! One tried to bite my poppa!
For the sea-gull is an independent bird.

If you feed a rotten carrot
To a mynah bird or parrot,
He may greet it with a most unpleasant word;
But the gull will whoop and hollar
Like a guy that's found a dollar,
For the sea-gull is an independent bird.

Where the Swedish coast-line glitters
Gulls are eating apple fritters
(The Swedes love apple fritters, so I've heard),
But here on Danish soil
They gulp gin and motor oil –
Now, isn't that an independent bird?

ST. FRANCIS AND THE SKEPTICS

St. Francis of Assisi, growing bored
With those who shunned the teachings of the Lord,
Set out one eve across the dewy vales
And preached a sermon to the nightingales.
They listened, charmed, beneath the moon's eclipse,
At the sweet words which fell from the Francis' lips,
And huddled, twittering, while the warming flow
Of eloquence set all the woods aglow.

Alone, an owl, annoyed, raised its head
And at the Saint cried "WHO?" and went to bed.
Nor would it rouse when Francis termed it "friend"
And told it of those joys which transcend
In Paradise. But as the Saint more loud
Did pray, and turned upon the crowd
Of shivering birds his apostolic ire,
The owl again screamed "WHO?" and to the spire
Of a far distant church escaped, there to remain
While good St. Francis called to it in vain.

Then, when the night her misty cloak did lift,
St. Francis sermonized the daylight shift—
Sparrows and jays and wrens with fluted bills,
White-breasted thrushes, crows and whippoorwills.
Intent upon his text, the birds in awe
Were silent at the beauty of God's law—
Save for a magpie that with strident screech
Exclaimed repeated against his speech,
And harshly whistled, hopped about and squalled
'Till from the din the poor Saint stopped, appalled.

Then to the sea he strode and spoke to gulls
And terns that nested in the rotting hulls
Of sailing ships, and herons dignified
That stood serenely in the swirling tide.
All civilly attended to his talk—
The bright-eyed snipe and crane, the watchful hawk,
The gaunt flamingo flaming in the dawn—
So that the beach became a silver lawn
Where aerial listeners heard divine discourse.
(O the quiet reverence of the albatross!)
Then suddenly, with flapping wings askew,
A pelican across the sand dunes flew,
And hurtling to the water with a swish,
Ignored a glimpse of heaven to gobble fish!

Thus Francis learned the new but useful creed—
That skeptics are a universal breed!

THE BARBER'S DAY OFF

"Hair cut?" The barber gently asked.
No answer made the ape.
But in some fancied magazine
Of Hollywood's new movie queen
Admired the luscious shape.

"Shampoo?" The barber raised his tone.
The ape gave no reply,
But with a long, uneasy nail
Brushed dandruff from his curling tail
And heaved a heavy sigh.

"Shave?" On the quiet, sunny air
The word hung like a bell.
But still the ape in sullen mood
His vagrant private thoughts pursued
As flees the light gazelle.

"Hot Towel?" The barber's voice grew rough
With mingled spite and rage.
The ape poked skinny fingers through –
For this was Sunday at the zoo –
The grating of his cage.

THE GOLDEN FLEECE

A young reporter, beastly drunk
Asked of the ram with golden fleece:
"But why – when Jason bobbed your locks –
Did you not scream for the police?"

Then answered with annoyed growl
The ram with fleece of finest gold:
"I seldom raise a futile howl.
Besides, I wasn't very cold.

"Have you forgot or did you know
That Jason, called the Argonaut,
Enveloped me with woolen shawls,
And knitted scarves which he had brought?"

"In Colchis, too, the golden rule
Was always practiced by our flock.
The dragons and the pretty girls
Went out to tea at five o'clock."

"But, why," the young reporter asked,
"Did you" – The ram with dreadful roar
Cried: "Go and ask the lamb of God!
I can't be bothered any more!"

THE GOOD SLEEP

A soulful sloth on pretzels fed
In his Elizabethan bed.
He wore pajamas mauve and pale
To match the glass of ginger ale
Which, raising gently to his lip,
He would occasionally sip.

A clock struck 12. In accents low
The sloth observed: "That clock is slow!"
He pulled the bedclothes in a heap
And turned around and fell asleep.
He slept and slept day after day,
And still inert and prone he lay.

Then down the street with sudden clang
Fire engines raced. The sloth's bell rang.
"Joe!" voices cried. "Your roof's on fire.
Joe! Joe! Wake up!"
The sloth in ire
Blinked stupidly and, with a frown,
Exclaimed: "Shut up! I won't come down."

"Be off! I'm tired. Go 'way! Desist!
Please run along! You won't be missed!"
But still they banged. One gave a shout:
"He's drunk, the fool. He won't come out."
The roof caved in. An icy stream
Of water struck the window beam.

The sloth exposed a sleepy eye
And saw the fireman running by.
"O Lord!" he groaned. "It's sad to think
One cannot catch a well-earned wink
Of sleep without some dreadful bore
Shouting and wetting up the floor!"

Then, as the flames he did discern,
He shrugged and muttered:
"Let 'er burn!"

The fireman, breaking down a wall,
Found him in ashes—Bed and all!

The Hippo With Political Ambitions

Beneath the sweet pajama trees
A baby hippo sat at ease
And dreamed about the gala day
When he from Africa would stray.
His present life appeared a grind
Unsuited to a cultured mind.
He found his dull companions heavy
And hippo maidens but a bevy
Of overnourished, idle blondes
Who floated 'round on lily ponds.
In future years he saw himself
With books upon the shelf
A girl whose hips were slightly narrow,
A clever son who went to Harrow,
But most of all to him seemed dear
A bright political career.

While thus he mused some hunters set
A trap and caught him in their net.
In fact, no sooner had they got him
Than they'd have very promptly shot him
Had not Sir Percy Whipple spied
A certain value to his hide
Quite unrelated to the term
Applied by a commercial firm.
Sir Percy liked the hippo's air
Of calm, magnificent despair,
The way his head was lifted high
Despite the moisture in his eye.
His bellow – vibrant as a klaxon –
Appeared distinctly Anglo-Saxon
And, issuing from that mighty gorge,
Recalled tirades of Lloyd George.

When back to England he returned,
With shocked surprise all London learned
That Whipple, the zoologist
Knighted in last year's birthday list,
Was haunting clubs in West End sections
With a great beast of vague connections.
Most horrified were all his friends.
The glamor that a hippo lends,
They felt, was no excuse to reach a
Camaraderie with such a creature.
Sir Percy's wife sued for divorce
After her husband bought a horse
And cantered along Rotten Row
With the monstrosity in tow.
After the break-up of his marriage
He lodged the hippo at the Claridge.

Years passed and passing brought a change.
The hippo that had once seemed strange
At formal teas, was now a pet
Among the most exclusive set.
With dukes the monster potted grouse
And had been dined at Marlborough House;
Indeed, one season had been sent
By liberals to Parliament,
But soon retired from elocution
Ruins a hippo's constitution.
At last, discouraged by the tricks
And knaveries of politics
Though Whipple (now Lord Whippletree)
Argued one night 'till half-past three
The noble animal once more
Set sail for Africa's dark shore.

Beneath the sweet pajama trees
This ancient hippo lies at ease
And ruminates on life and fate
To twenty children and a mate.
The secret of success, says he,
Is not to roam beyond the sea
But to remain extremely quiet
While practicing a breadfruit diet.
On politics he does not gloat;
He'd like to send his sons to Choate.
He thinks no woman can eclipse
His two-ton wife's enormous hips.
The youngest of his husky boys
Sulks frequently among his toys.
He dreams of girls whose hips are narrow
And plans some day to go to Harrow,
Though most of all to him seems dear
His Dad's political career!

THE IMPORTANCE OF PROTOCOL

The keeper of a modern zoo
Must be possessed of social tact.
He bows discreetly to The Gnu;
He shows Leaf Monkeys how to act;
He slips The Lion chocolate creams;
He daily fills The Hippo's tub;
Nor would he in his wildest dreams
Omit The Rhino's beauty rub.

Charles Herman Sophocles O'Toole
Was such a keeper, and his fame
In stressing diplomatic rule
Is indicated by his name.
The furnished collar for Giraffe
And boxing gloves for Kangaroo;
He made the bored Hyena laugh –
He was the hero of his Zoo!

And yet, how sad that after all
O'Toole contrived the Zoo to cheer,
One single error caused his fall
And ended a superb career!
Yes, only once did he by chance
The laws of PROTOCOL repulse
And bar The Zebra's striped pants
With unforeseeable results!

This Zebra was a trifle fey
And to pomposity inclined.
He wore his stripes the self-same way
He wore his very simple mind.
So, when the Zoologic School
Gave for the animals a dance
The Zebra bluntly asked O'Toole
If he might wear some striped pants.

"It would," said he, "be ultra-chic
And, also help the woolen trade
To amplify my fine physique
With stripes by human tailors made."
Replied the Keeper: "Trade in wool
Does not depend on how you're dressed.
Your natural stripes look linen cool.
I must say 'no' to your request."

Around the fashion conscious Zoo
The gossip ran like trouser-cuffs.
There'd never been such a to-do
Since they'd abolished Tudor ruffs.
The Tiger, though he sometimes roared
For Zebra steak (the greedy rogue!)
In angry diatribe deplored
That stripes no longer were in vogue.

"Next, spots," The Leopard snarled, "are out.
Such is the latest O'Toole code.
Unless we all rebel and shout
Soon Billy Goat will be the mode."
Up rose The Jaguar and The 'Coon.
Up sprang each wild zebraic colt.
The Zebra went into a swoon,
And all the Zoo went in revolt.

The Porcupine with muted whine
Speared at O'Toole a well-aimed quill.
The Grizzly Bear with ursine glare
Growled: "Crush him like a dollar bill."
In berserk rage, from every cage
The beasts of tooth and claw advance...
Thus, died the Keeper of the Zoo –
All on account of striped pants.

If some day, Chiefs of Protocol,
Your servile Diplomatic Corps
Should like The Zebra (poor dull soul!)
Some tiny boon from you implore
Look not askance at striped pants!
Be not as stubborn as a mule!
'Ere ye say 'nay' remember pray
Charles Herman Sophocles O'Toole!

THE MAID'S DAY OUT

"Does that animal bite?" asked the Duchess one night
On the Orpington-Smiths' palm veranda.
She nodded her head, with a shudder of dread,
Toward the tiger they'd brought from Uganda.

"Oh, heavens, dear Duchess," said Orpington-Smith.
"Old Brindle is tame as a kitten.
The story that tigers are fierce is a myth
Invented by one who was bitten."

"The secret is food. If you fatten 'em good
All tigers grow meek as a moppet.
Old Brindle each day gets a chocolate soufflé...
Who, Brindle! – Down, Brindle – Hey STOP IT!"

Mrs. Orpington-Smith from her knitting arose.
"I thought that old Brindle looked thinner."
She gave a great shout: "It's the new maid's day out.
The damn fool's FORGOTTEN HIS DINNER!!!"

THE MAROONED MONKEY

On an island of mangos, mimosa and musk,
With a coastline uncomfortably sandy,
And old marooned monkey sat drinking at dusk
From a bottle of Portuguese brandy.

He'd been drunk for a week on this horrible beach,
Half dazed by the screeching of parrots
Plus a whole case of brandy convenient to reach,
Washed ashore with a bushel of carrots.

A stranger forlorn to all tropical monks
Was this monkey who lived in a city,
For he had been born in a cage at the Bronx
And been wrecked on a trip to Tahiti.

He gazed through the dusk with his pitiful eyes
At a white speck that gleamed in the ocean,
Then suddenly screamed unintelligible cries
And wept with unwonted emotion.

He fished out the speck and he brought it to shore
('Twas nothing but water-logged paper)
And drank two more bottles of brandy before
Passing out with a monkeyshine caper.

Now, the curious fact (I regard it with awe),
Is that when by a Jap expedition
The monk's bones were found, he held clutched in one paw
The New York Times Sunday edition.

THE MONKEY CURE

In a tall royal palm on the side of a hill
Lay two little monkeys both dreadfully ill.
One had the measles, the other had flu.
Their doctor was baffled to know what to do.
He ordered them beaten with coconut rope;
He scared them by threatening an elegant hearse--
And still the two monkeys grew steadily worse.

The specialists came (the two monkeys had money)
And quickly prescribed a transfusion of honey
Plus a strange scarlet juice – twenty dollars an ounce –
With a name which the experts could scarcely pronounce.
But, alas, with their doctors' bills high as the skies,
The poor monkeys temperatures, too, took a rise.
The relatives rolled in like volcanic lava.
A cable was sent to an uncle in Java.
Five spatulate cousins arrived from Brazil,
All hoping 'gainst hope to be named in the will.

A last desperate gamble! Sir Timothy Monk
Blew in with a mouse in an old steamer trunk.
He opened the lip. Although ready to die,
The invalids lifted an indolent eye.
"What's that?" they inquired, as the mouse gave a squeak.
They jumped from their bed and weren't seen for a week.
"They are cured!" cried the doctors. "'Twas only a chill."
"They are cured!" groaned the rest and returned to Brazil.
"We are cured!" yelled the invalids, doing a jive.
"Excitement's the magic that keeps us alive!"

THE WAITER AND THE ALLIGATOR

Beneath the muck and mud
Of the Mississippi flood
Lies the alligator.
Behind the potted plants
Of Parisian restaurants
Lurks the waiter.

With his elongated teeth
He will eat you like roast beef,
Will the alligator.
With his sickly little grin
He will scoop your money in,
Will the waiter.

If I had to choose between
The crocodile and Paris green
And the waiter,
I'd take the poison off the bat
And after that
The alligator.

THE WEEPING SHEEP

One day I met a weeping sheep.
"For whom," I asked him, "do you weep?"
He bleated: "For the human race,"
And tears ran down his foolish face.

I never used to give a damn
When I saw people eating lamb,
But now my circulation stops
At the mere whiff of mutton chops.

TRIUMPH OF THE COW

PHILADELPHIA, May 19— "Discovery of a method whereby
alcohol may be extracted from milk was announced here today."
...NEWSPAPER ITEM

O Guernsey with the dove-like eyes!
O Hersey with the ample thighs!
O Holstein with the spotted flanks,
Accept my very heartfelt thanks!
Now, when at breakfast I appear
(it happens once or twice a year)
Shall I not have – O yet who browse! –
Gin rickeys from contented cows?

What do I care what dish I eat –
Flakes, crispies, grape nuts, cream 'o wheat,
Eggs poached or boiled or shirred or fried,
Bacon or sausage on the side,
Coffee or chocolate, tea or cream?
To hell with these! My only dream
Is to discover smooth as silk
A trace of whiskey in the milk.

What infant Hercules shall thrill
To bourbon in his daily swill,
And many-headed hydras throttle
After a ship at his new bottle?
Alas, poor nurse who tries to quiet
A baby on a whiskey diet!

Only a genius in whom burn
Hangover memories could turn
Breakfast, after a hectic night
Into an epicure's delight.
Just picture drinks with raptures sly
Munching corn muffins made of rye!

Disheartening, though, it is to think
How some will treat this latest drink;
For certain persons, fond of punch,
Will order only milk for lunch,
While creatures of the lowest ilk
Will gulp a double buttermilk!

WAITING FOR LEFTY

"Dress, white tie. It is considered appropriate to send out drinks to
the thirsty coachmen, but not to the horses."

—Protocol briefing for the American Ambassador to the
Court of Saint James's calling on Her Majesty the Queen...

Foggy and black is the London night
But Buckingham Palace gleams with light,
Each time its doors are opened wide
Music pours on the ones outside.

A line of coaches is waiting there,
Stretching as far as Berkeley Square
(Or almost). Anyhow, there they wait,
Horses and Coachmen, such as fate.

The coachmen sit in their bright cockades,
Sipping whiskies and lemonades,
Orange sherberts and French champagne
With a touch of Schnapps (against fog and rain).

And what do their patient horses get,
Standing there, in the cold and wet,
Nostrils flaring and ears a-flap?
"Give 'im a touch o' the whip, old chap!"

Inside, they're cutting capers and cake;
Outside, the horses shiver and shake;
Inside, it's burgundy zero two;
Outside, the coachmen are guzzling too.

O what a soft if sad refrain!
An English horse in an English rain;
A fat, sleek coachman drunk on the box;
And only the fog around for blocks!

WASHINGTONIA

A Political Campaign in the Johnson Era

Two candidates for Congress ran –
Orestes Henry Bones,
A pleasant, smiling sort of man,
And Mulligatawny Jones.

You'll seldom spy as grim a guy
As Mulligatawny Jones,
His look was sad, his breath was bad.
He spoke in raucous tones.

While Bones would kiss and cuddle babes,
Jones swilled at every bar.
Bones' manner was like Honest Abe's
Before the Civil War.

He soothed his hosts with artful toasts
While speaking on Viet-Nam,
Jones snarls and snorts drew sharp retorts,
He didn't give a damn.

He used smear tricks of politics,
His jokes were crude and corny.
He sneaked and schemed. No project seemed
Too low for Mulligatawny.

Election day dawned cold and wet,
And busy buzzed the phones
As every wise election bet
Buzzed strong for Mr. Bones.

The train pulled into Washington
And stopped there with a jerk.
The jerk got off, walked up the Hill
And Congress went to work.

Now was it Jones or was it Bones
Who beat the other flat?
Why, Bones, God wot, for was he not
A Johnson Democrat?

A RULE OF PROTOCOL

The first thing to learn – on this we insist –
Is how to make a smart protocol list.
You don't select men of distinction or brain.
Choose dumbbells who cannot come out of the rain.
No scientist, doctor or artist of note,
Not even a gent in a well-tailored coat.
Forget about Green books or Forbes or Who's Whos;
Just pick out some name from the evening news.

Suppose that a foreign King visits our shores
And we give him a dinner... Be sure that the bores,
The dopes, the nonentities all are on hand.
Be equally sure that all talent is banned.
Drag any old crow from his usual haunts;
Don't get a guest that His Majesty wants.

A hair-dresser fired by Elizabeth Arden,
A shyster awaiting the governor's pardon,
A broken-down crooner named Gumbulch or Zeke,
A labor thug voting in Brooklyn next week,
Some dubious lady society-slighted –
All these must – repeat <u>must</u> be promptly invited!

So follow this rule! To no side issue yield,
And you'll be a star in the protocol field.

An Old Aristrocratic Dinner in Washington

The dining room – Georgian;
The atmosphere – formal;
The wine list – Borgian;
The guest list – subnormal.

The chandelier – Venice;
The silver – old English;
The butler – old menace;
The lady next me – tinglish.

The soup – "tortue claire";
The veal – "Milanese";
The host – very "savoir faire";
The hostess – plumb crazy.

The jewels – magnificent;
The liqueurs – none better;
The cigars – reminiscent;
The house pet – a setter.

The start – young and bright;
The mid-meal – a question;
The later-on – old and tight;
The end – indigestion!

ATTACK OF THE TROLLS AT AN EMBASSY PARTY

Perhaps it's that third musician...
Perhaps it's the pain in my head...
Oh, I know it's only illusion,
But I wish that the trolls were dead!

They are weaving a horrible carpet
Under the emerald hill,
A brilliant, moon-drenched carpet
With needles of daffodil...
(God, how my head keeps throbbing!
If only that music were still...)

Weaving and dancing, those troll-folk,
Tiny and vicious and cold,
With beady, lascivious pig-eyes
In faces a thousand years old...

Hist! Can't you hear that screaming?
(The gnomes and the leprechaun can.)
'Tis the scream of the furious troll-folk
Against their great enemy-man!
(Give me another whiskey...
I'll forget the trolls and their clan.)

Tra la la! Tra la la! They are pacing
A weird and loathsome gavotte
To the click of their saffron-hued needles,
While hatching a terrible plot.

They have finished their horrible carpet,
Glistening, obscene and vile...
They swarm from the emerald hill-top
Mile upon mile upon mile.

Crawling and creeping and screaming,
Holding their carpet unfurled
To spread its shimmering meshes
Over a horror-struck world...
(For God's sake... gimme a whiskey...
The trolls!... The Trolls!... THE TROLLS!!!!)

DEAR LITTLE GIRL

On a pleasant August evening
Henry Aiken's little niece
Asked the telephone exchange how
She could dial the police.
To the operator's questions
She retorted clear but low:
"I've murdered Uncle Henry, and
I think they ought to know!"

GEORGETOWN RHAPSODY

Dear Georgetown, I love you!
Your gables all leak—
Your ceilings are plastic—
Your women lack chic—
Your tax is outrageous—
Your champagne is warm—
So what's your contagious,
Peculiar charm?

Your cables and crinkles
Have bored me for years—
Your candle-light twinkles
On hippies and queers—
You rave of your artists—
(A glorious list!)
But strictly between us,
They'd never be missed.

Your over-priced galleries,
Your over-stuffed shirts,
Your over-sexed kids are
So dreadful it hurts.
Then why do I love you?
I haven't a clue,
Unless it could be I'm
As stupid as you!

GIVE THE OLD LADY A PAINT-BRUSH!

Give the old lady a paint-brush, Oscar!
And some beefsteak to put on that eye!
She looks like a painting by Moses,
So timid an' bashful an' shy?

She comes here for Sunday luncheon,
Sweet an' perky an' neat,
Peppermint goodies crunchin'
Little green shoes on her feet.

Hummin' an air from La Tosca,
Little red rose in her hair –
And what do you do to her, Oscar?
You knock her down with a chair!

Give the old lady a paint-brush, Oscar!

HANGOVER

Brightness explodes and in an aching shower spills
All the sounds of morning over me......
Birds, a distant phone, a far-off TV symphony,
Someone knocking at the door.
Harsh white sunshine usurps and fills
The void of blackness, stabs at my ankle
With a stiletto of anguish......

I grope my way to the bathroom......
Like shiny surgical instruments
The plumbing fixtures gleam
Hygienically......
Torture devices from a sadist's dream,
All so clean, so neat, so painful!...

In the Library of Congress...an Old Roman Menu

Great Ceasar's ghost! What sort of host
Would throw such orgies fabulous?
The only kind that comes to mind
Is maybe Heliogabalus!

Stewed lampreys! Nightingales in snow!
Flamingos' tongues in honey!
No, no! – And skip that curried crow!
Just give me back my money!

I am not keen on roasted dog
Or sheeps' eyes dipped in jelly,
While filet of Phoenician frog
Seems frankly "causus belli!"

A crude barbarian am I
In gastronomic journeyin'.
I'll drain my whiskey goblet dry.
To hell with your Falernian!

MOMENTS IN THE WASHINGTON MONUMENT

I climbed the monument steps –
Six hundred and eighty-eight –
(Or is it eight hundred and sixty-six?
I never <u>can</u> get it straight!)

At any rate, I climbed them,
Cloppity-cloppity-clop!!!
Until with the thrill of exhaustion
I reached the very top.

Picknickers, Mummies, Daddies,
People with paper bags,
Tourists with kids and kodaks,
Young girls and ancient hags –

"How does one jump from a window?"
I asked a passing guard.
He looked at me like a zombie
And answered, "The windows are barred."

"We don't allow window jumping,
This is a moral town."
"You walked up? You wasted your time, Bud!
Just take the lift to go down!"

OBSERVATION ON STATE DEPARTMENT PERSONALITIES

As a watcher who observes
The constant war of nerves
Existing in our present situation,
I have noted with concern
That at State they seldom learn –
Perhaps a rather caustic observation.

But when one probes more deep
Where the lacquered lizards creep
There comes to one a sudden revelation:
It is simply that at State
They're completely second rate –
You might term it an empirical equation.

ON A VISTA OF THE PORTUGUESE EMBASSY LAUNDRY

My window faces hills and lawns
Where doubtless little leprechauns
Get drunk at night on acorn cups
Brimming with Autumn wine.
I also see beneath the trees
The laundry which the Portuguese
Have hung within unself-conscious ease
Along a fluttery line.

One wonders does the butler wear
Those mauve pajamas shimmering there
Or does their rich, exotic flair
Imply a higher rank?
And will those socks (a number ten?)
Adorn the feet of gentlemen
Who'll grace a dance at the U.N.
With diplomatic swank?

And can Her Excellency squirm
Into those panties? Can she worm
Her hefty hips into their firm
But useful looking mesh?
Or does some slender, slinky maid,
Quite unabashed and undismayed,
Fit snugly to th' encircling braid
Her palpitating flesh?

O visions, visions! Here I stand
Like one in fabled Samarkand,
Enchanted as Balboa and
As silent too as he.

God bless the worthy Portuguese
Who – aided by the morning breeze –
Have furnished such delights as these
To daze and dazzle me!

PRECEDENCE

The Protocol Chief shook his silvery locks.
"I'm sorry," he said, "But it's so.
"Everyone understands that it's out of my hands –
Just a protocol rule, don't you know!"

The Ambassador took up his pearl-headed stick,
Assumed an appearance of gloom;
Then bowed to his host, struck his heels with a click
And stalked with aplomb from the room.

He walked like a man in a sleep-walker's daze
To the lift with its cage open wide.
Without half a look at the chances he took,
He stepped nonchalantly inside.

Since the lift wasn't there – though the gate stood ajar –
He fell several floors to his death.
"I was placed by a Balt, far below any salt",
He explained with his last gasp of breath.

PRESTIGE IN WASHINGTON

He had no sense of humor
And he suffered from a tumor
And there was a dreadful rumor
Of the way his nights were spent—
But he knew a man whose brother
Was married to the mother
Of a gal who had a special pal
Who knew the President.

His laugh was never hearty
And his face was pocked and warty,
Yet to every single party
He invariably went—
For wasn't it his cousin
Who controlled an even dozen
Of Senators whose buzzin'
Had intrigued the President?

He was flatter than a waffle;
He was boring, dismal, awful;
He practiced tricks unlawful
With felonious intent—
But his son had some connections
And political affections
In high echelon directions
That attract the President.

So he had to be invited,
And his hosts were quite delighted,
Though their kindness he requited
To a laughable extent—
Because it seems this joker
Had won large sums at poker
From the father of the broker
Who financed the President.

PROTOCOL WILL GET YOU

(apologies to JWR)

On a hot and humid night when you just can't sleep –
Counting stupid dividends instead of stupid sheep –
And worry over diplomats and what your friends have said,
And know they'll never think of you one day when you are dead –
Get up and dress, got to a bar, and give some guy a clout
'Cause <u>Protocol</u> will get you if you don't watch out!

When you sit at dinner by a sexy-looking gal
And realize she is, in fact, a Russian agent's pal,
Don't smile at her politely and toast her health in fizz,
Just ask her very bluntly how the spying business is!
Alarm your host and hostess with a terrifying shout,
'Cause <u>Protocol</u> will get you if you don't watch out!

At a white tie function make your own tie black.
Come there on a scooter! Don't use a Cadillac!
Glower at the butler – toss the maid your coat.
Ask about the ranking guest: "<u>Who</u> is that old goat?"
As to what you think of him, don't leave a single doubt –
'Cause <u>Protocol</u> will get you if you don't watch out!

When the dry martini glitters in the glass
And you see a diplomat start to make a pass
At a new ambassadress – tell him who is whom
Don't wait 'til her husband's in the other room.
Run and tell him instantly what it's all about –
'Cause <u>Protocol</u> will get you if you don't watch out!

RAINY GEORGETOWN WEEKEND

Here I lie, invitations scorning,
Hugging the fire, in my Georgetown flat.
Nothing to do until Monday morning
Nothing to stroke but an old Brooks hat.

What do I see thru my window curtain?
A cleaning woman – she cleans real nice.
Rain in the gutter. Two poor, uncertain
Pansy pussycats chasing mice.

A girl in pajamas munching taffy,
A dope who leans on a garden rake,
An old, deaf Senator, party daffy,
Writing a speech that he'll never make.

Nothing to read but a sexy novel
That drew the Bishop of York's reproof,
Nothing but squeaks from a cracked steam shovel
And rain that starts to drum on the roof.

REH PINSCHER SPECTERS

My two dogs,
Like two logs,
Lie and snore
On the floor.
And they sigh
As they lie,
And each nose
In repose
Seems to twitch
With an itch
That declares:
"Oh, those hares!
How they leap
As we creep
Through our dream!
How they gleam
Mid the grass
As we pass,
To our woe,
Sad and slow,
For we can't –
Though we pant –
Quite keep up!"

Thus, each pup
Feels harassed
And outclassed.
Thus, his ear
Seems to hear
Crackling leaves.
He believes
That he jumps
Over stumps;
That he trails

After quails;
That he sees
Through the trees
Such a feast
As a beast
Might surmise
Paradise!

Yet his paws
Fail, because
As he yaps
And he snaps
And he growls
And he howls,
Weights of lead
Slow his tread,
While a clamp
As of damp
Iron hands
Grasps like bands
'Til his girth
Brushes earth.

Ah, what chance
To romance
On the theme
Of this dream!
Forests dark
Where a bark
Is a prayer!
Where disrepair
Holds her reign!
Yet this twain
Of chasseurs –
Two poor curs –

Bravely fights
Like twin knights
Against plot
And what not!
They would fly
Through the sky!
They would skim
Through the dim,
Dismal vales,
Wagging tails!
Though delayed,
Unafraid,
They pursue
(Pray, would you?)
Phantom game.

Shall I blame
Then, their snarls?
A King Charles
May behave
As a brave
St. Bernard
In a yard,
And a Peke
His physique
May admire –
In a byre.
Every breed

At his need
Has his day,
So they say.
Maybe these
Find surcease
Of their life
In this strife.
They may feel
Strong as steel,
And may say
With each bay:
"Please observe
We have nerve.
We are scions
Of lions,
All tawny
And brawny.
We are strong.
You are wrong
To presume
We'd resume
Our old life –
Free of strife,
(If we could),
And be good
Like oodles
Of poodles."

THE BIG IDEA

"Mrs. Mesta said that she thought an American Museum should have American Indians, standing around at the opening. So. Mrs. Glenn Emmons, wife of the Commissioner of Indian Affairs, started scouting around."

The Washington Post

March 15, 1968

Big Chief Bald Eagle had received the bad news,
So he called in the Council to give them his views.
There was Rain-in-the-Washbasin, stolid and grim,
And Running Wolf looking quite wolfish and slim,
And Chief Happy Hunting, who was subject to fits,
And frightened the Palefaces out of their wits,
And Green-Feather-Moonshine, who drank lemonade
And was painted a beautiful lavender shade.

The Chiefs sat and pondered and gazed at the fire
With eyes quite devoid of human desire.
They smoked and they grunted and twiddled their toes.
They looked at each other. Bald Eagle arouse,
And addressing the gathering, he said: "Ugg-a Grugg!
Ugg! Rugger! Ugg! Bugger! Agulugger! Ugg! Glugg!"
Which being translated, I frankly confess,
Means simple: "This goddamn idea is a mess!"

"You mean it's a Mesta," grinned Moonshine the Creek,
Who'd studied at Yale and could even talk Greek.
But silence fell bleakly. The joke was bad taste.
Bald Eagle stared at the scalp at his waist,
And grunted: "More joking like that, my dear friend,
And in Tomahawk Valley you'll probably end.
We can't afford levity... Who in the hell
Are we going to send Mesta? Ummph!... Big Chiefs, please tell!"

Then some said a Seminole, practiced and sly,
With a snake up his sleeve and a glint in his eye.
"But suppose that he goosed – No, I cannot go on,"
Bald Eagle retorted. "No, it just isn't done!
We'll pick a cheap Indian, a Crow or a Kaw,
Unversed in diplomacy, finesse or law,
But solemn and proper, who knows what to do...
I guess after all we must send her a Sioux."

The Chiefs nodded slowly and puffed at the pipe;
And Moonshine, incorrigible, gave a loud "Yipe!"
"Yes, yes," he cried. "Chiefs, it's the one thing to do.
If you sent her an Osage I'm sure she would Sioux."
The meeting broke up with a series of whoops
And Running Wolf raced in a whirlwind of loops.
Big Chief Bald Eagle groaned: "What's the use?
Today a big Indian chief's just a papoose.
He goes to museums – Ummph! What a disgrace!
When ordered by Perle-Arden-Mud-in-the-Face!"

THE DECLINE OF ELEGANCE

His clothes were cut by Savile Row,
His gloves by Horace Sleep.
His tweedy pleats drew frightened bleats
From most exclusive sheep.

His ties of silk from Gucci came,
His polished boots from Peal
That caused low moans from baritones
Whose shoes had Sax-appeal.

Each month an alligator died
In order not to botch
The strap that held his unexcelled
Gold Patek Philippe watch.

Alas, Beau Brummel's day is dead
As yesterday's desire!
No modern guy can long defy
An unpaid tailor's ire.

Our friend discovered that instead
Of fur-lined overcoats
He was supplied on every side
With curt, demanding notes.

He had to shun the paneled shops
With bows and opened doors
In place of Sulka rose the bulk 'o
Cut-rate clothing stores.

His ties from Gimbel's bargain sale
Attracted sullen looks
And shocked the staid with readymade
Accessories from Brooks.

He sank to wearing checkered suits
With aquascutum vest,
And Macy's name replaced the fame
Of Hawes & Curtis's best.

He sank and sank til he was stripped
Down to his final dollar.
One sad July he had to buy
(O Christ!) an Arrow collar.

They found him in Hart Schaffner short
Roused by the landlord's shout.
But 'ere he died he'd reached inside
And torn the label out.

THE FOREIGN POLICY OF BOORA BOO

The policy of Anakanda Loo,
For many years the Chief of Boora Boo,
Was simply with the Spaniards to act skittish,
To shock the French and to annoy the British.
For this he kept his men supplied with knives,
Drugs, liquor, firearms and seductive wives,
A cellar full of dusty Bordeaux wines,
Twelve cobras and a score of concubines.

The Spanish Minister objected to
This policy of Anakanda Loo
Who frequently, insultingly made plain
He had no use at all for Franco's Spain.
The French, although his wines they found were good,
Old Anakanda Loo misunderstood.
When, to distress the French Ambassador,
He snubbed his wife, then made a pass at her,
The French declared the Chief not "comme il faut"
And wired De Gaulle their hopes that he would go.

Alone the British, zealous for their mission,
Kept carrying on their great Empire tradition.
The cricket fields of Eton in their view
Became the dismal swamps of Boora Boo.
'Though snubbed and sneered at, booed and put to shame,
They wore their dinner jackets just the same,
When Anakanda threw a dinner party
The British went, all starched and pink and hearty.
A cobra crept in, poisonously sinister,
And 'neath the table bit the English Minister.
The Foreign Office criticized the snake
But cabled it was merely a mistake
They selfishly regretted. In a hurry
They sent another Minister from Surrey.

The policy of Anakanda Loo
For many years brought him rich revenue.
But life is strange, especially in climes
Like Boora Boo in stirring modern times.
A revolution overthrew the Chief
And Anakanda Loo went on relief.
His nephew, Kandalooka, who seized power,
Tossed out the hated French within the hour,
Exiled the British raj, explaining why:
An Englishman gave B. B. snakes the evil eye.
As for the Spaniards – well, in Boora Boo
They proved less popular than Spanish flu.

Yet Kandalooka, raging against Europe,
Dosed flurried foreigners with soothing syrup.
He once had seen New York and since that day
Had very much admired the U.S.A.
He opened, when he could, negotiation
For diplomatic parlays with our nation.
All Boora Boolans touchingly displayed
A fond desire for economic aid.

The Kandalooka policy indeed
Proved pro-American, pro-progress and pro-speed.
His guests have Coca Cola and ice-cream
And Cadillacs (the Boora-Boolan's dream!)
He's killed the cobras in the palace cellar.
His wife gets all her clothers from Bonwit Teller.
In democratic fashion Kandalooka
Has bought from us a very fine bazooka
With which to put down any insurrection
From his young cousin, Dalnakian's direction.

Because, alas, it seems that dirty cuss,
Dalnakian, is not fond of us,
And there are even persons who declare
He's playing footsie with the Russian bear

That promises relief from sweat and toil
If he will sell aluminum and oil.
Ah, could one understand (dear friend, can you?)
The foreign policy of Boora Boo
One might perhaps know whether one should deal
In threats or promises or love or steel,
Or fling one's arms around a new-found brother
Or urge two petty chiefs to kill each other!
Millennium may come. Why should we fret?
One thing is for sure – it has not happened yet.
Until it comes we still must sell bazookas
To boors and Boora Boos and Kandalookas.

THE GHOSTLY TOAST OF WASHINGTON

When all the heavenly armies marched in splendor
Against Beelzebub, legion upon legion of Angels –
The twelfth Seraphim division and the bugle corps of Cherubs,
Included – pennants unfurled and the bright arms
Flashing back the glory of the spheres,
Mr. B. Z. Jones sat in his library, considering.
He badly wanted a job with the administration.
But who had the most influence? The Angels? Beelzebub?
He couldn't find the answer to that question.
He had not been a good man – nor a very bad one.
The postman took a glass of sherry with him at Christmas.
His name was in the green book. He adored Bach
Played at midnight by a girl in a diaphanous nightie.
So what? Wasn't he still on the side of the Angels?

Or was he? His hand fell upon a book of Black Magic,
Esoteric but stupid stuff. Medieval, passe. Still,
Even passe devils have pull.
Mr. B. Z. Jones wished that he could have a sign, a vision.
He sat in his library considering what to do.
Should he send a little message to Archangel Michael?
They had met briefly at FDR's funeral.
Or maybe invite Beelzebub to a stag dinner?
Then something passed in front of the lamp, cold and slippery,
And someone stood warming his hands at Mr. Jones's fire.
"Cold night tonight, Bee-Zee!" said the visitor.
He laughed pleasantly,
Stamping a bit of snow on the rug. Why didn't it melt?
Mr. Jones wondered. Without saying anything he walked over,
Bent down and touched the snow. It was not snow at all.
It was white pearls glowing in the firelight.

"A neat trick!" commented Mr. Jones. His visitor laughed again.

"Shucks" he said. That's nothing at all. "Look at this."

He shook his head and a lot of papers fell out of his hair.

Mr. Jones picked one up. "My God," he gasped;

"This is the Constitution of the United States."

He picked up another, "A Congressional bill to turn the

Mississippi River into a duck pond for the enjoyment of

Wives and dependents of ex-service men!...

And this? A list of Southerners who voted against

Speaker Rayburn's plan to broaden the Rules Committee."

Mr. Jones felt like a blind piano-tuner who has missed B-sharp.

The inspiration hit him. "I know who you are," he cried.

"You're not God and you're not the Devil. You're the spirit of

Washington Politics!...You never die, no matter who wins.

To hell with Angels and Beelzebub. Sit down and have a drink!"

THE PASSIONATE EARS

(Portrait of a certain lady)

Her ears were sheathed in gold
And her nose was very cold
On my cheek
When we danced the Varsoviana
And I felt the icy glamor
Of her beak.

Her voice said "Sinatra";
Her hair-do "Cleopatra" –
In a way.
'Though what aroused my fears
Was what her golden ears
Didn't say.

Her throat was wreathed in scarabs
And the art of ancient Arabs
Ringed her arm,
While a touch of Tyrian dye
Encircling each bright eye
Let her charm.

But her throat and all the rest
(And perhaps – when she's undressed –
There is more)...
Cannot the mystery hold
Of those ear-muffs made of gold
Which she wore.

THE PEACOCK ROOM

One day, immersed in gorgeous gloom,
In Mr. Whistler's peacock room.
Where painted peacocks large and small
Cavort superbly on the wall,
This errant, nagging thought occurred
As I identified each bird:
If only Whistler had remained
In Washington and had disdained
To satirize the greedy bluff
Of clients who wouldn't pay enough,
But had determined to portray
Instead the statesmen of his day,
What plumes these peacocks could have spread!
On what strange corn would they have fed?

What murals could have best expressed
Garfield, McKinley and the rest
Who, scouting petty social feud,
Their aims to aimless death pursued?
These peacocks mock our mod physiques
With outflung wings and savage beaks
And waft us to that halcyon scene
When old Victoria was Queen...
More!... had the artist lived he might
Have here revealed a Roosevelt's plight,
A Harding's grief, a Hoover's pain,
A Coolidge picking golden grain!

THE PERFECT FIT

"Too fat to fit," the tailor said,
And sadly shook his grizzled head.
"For many a day, for many a year
I've fitted people from toe to ear,
I've fitted humans of every shape –
I've even fitted a stylish ape."
He shrugged. "I'd have to go to the zoo
And skin a hippo to cover you."

"Too foul to live," the client replied.
"I came to be fitted, not decried."
He seized some shears from a nearby rack
And plunged them into the tailor's back.
"Lengthen the sleeves, let out the waist.
Cut lapels to the wearer's taste!
Lower right shoulder – forget the price –
That teakwood coffin will fit real nice!"

THE POISONER

She does not gloat with gay, mad eyes
O'er rhapsodies of lead
Laced with the seeds of killer weeds
Filched from the gardener's shed.

Her poison is more subtle far
Than drips from any quill.
It makes harsh dents in common sense
And atrophies the will.

THE SENTIMENTALIST

He wept at a wedding; he winced at a wake;
At movies he cried loud and hard,
But greatest of all was the pleasure he'd take
From a dog-bone he'd found in the yard.

He mused: "They may call it a dog-bone, of course,
And yet it has color and charm.
Perhaps it's the rib of a primitive horse
From an antediluvian farm."

He polished the bone like a super-waxed floor,
Then carried it, cuddled in ice,
To one versed in anthropological lore
And asked his considered advice.

For hours the scientist prodded and probed
And panted with scholarly glee
'Til, lifting his head with a whimper, he said:
"It's just an old dog-bone to me."

"Oh, no," cried the finder. "Perchance it comes straight
From the corpse of a pleistocene man
That some sabretooth tiger with appetite ate
In the days of the pipe playing Pan."

"You mix anthropology, sir, with mythology,"
The scientist said. "You'll agree
Your theory's pure rot, for what you have got
Is just an old dog-bone, you see."

"No, no," screamed the other. He wrapped up the bone
In camphor and cotton and glue
And placed it himself on a green velvet shelf
For various experts to view.

Alas, an anonymous poodle escaped
With the bone from its velvet settee.
As he chewed it for lunch, he observed:
"Crunch! Crunch! Crunch!"
Which means: "It's a dog-bone to me!"

THE SOCIAL SUCCESS

He dined each night with old dull dames
Whose sagging double chins
Wagged back and forth – now West, now North –
Like painted fishes' fins.

He stroked their thin, bejeweled hands
And kissed their withered cheeks;
A hint of wine and turpentine
Adhered to him for weeks.

For this he claimed the doubtful gain
Of nibbling plovers' eggs
With diplomats who hung their hats
On State Department pegs.

Nor was he forced to pick each night
Salami from the fridge.
Soon every rich exclusive bitch
Invited him to bridge.

Of course, he had to suffer bores
So dreadfully intense
He often wept and sometimes slept
In candid self defense.

Wild invitations, pile on pile,
Cascaded through his door.
His postman cried: "It's suicide!"
They added one man more.

To carry wires and billets-doux
And cards with golden crest,
Plus plaintive pleas to lunch and teas
Ecstatically expressed.

He answered all – he went to all.
He went and went and went...
Soon he became a man of fame –
A social monument.

Then lo! One fatal day in June
He married Dotty Drear.
No class, no show, no chic, no dough –
Thus ended his career!

Today his muddy stream of mail
Contains no social bids.
Alone beside the telephone
He caters to his kids.

He winds up pussy-cats and trains
And clears up all the litter
Of cigarettes and racing bets
Left by the baby sitter.

He sadly rattles dominoes
(He's never asked to bridge!)
Until at six poor Dotty picks
Salami from the fridge.

THE SUN IS MY UNDOING

There is a charm, no doubt, in frozen lakes
Where through the stillness wails the plaintive loon
And a pale blob of Gorgonzola makes
What naïve natives call the Winter moon.

Yet frozen lakes so icy and refined,
With clear, clean ice—what are they, friend, but death?
Death's silver handled coffin, satin-lined?
Death's mirror marred by no outrageous breath?

Give me hot skies with their insulting blue
That turn to red your peeling Yankee nose,
And into air-conditioning your flue,
And into ridicule your heavy snows!

Give me a lush, responsive tropic belle
Whose generous lips betray a sensual mouth,
And bougainvillea playing scarlet hell
With old, decaying mansions of the South!

Give me that lazy, never-ending beach,
Those nights that swoon beneath uncounted stars,
And Spanish moss and owls that hoot and screech,
And the aroma of untaxed cigars!

Go take your lakes and ski boots, dog and gun!
I'm decadent, I'm dopey. Just leave me
My frangipani beauties and the sun
Burning gold velvet patterns on the sea!

WHAT PROTOCOL TAUGHT ME

I learned it was lese-majeste
A fresh idea to launch,
Though one could send the same old tripe
By diplomatic "paunch."
I learned that two and two make five
When drafting foreign notes,
And you could steal your colleagues' files
If not their overcoats.

I had supposed an aide-memoire
Meant really what it said,
But soon discovered it to be
A stumbling block instead.
I had presumed Ambassadors
A super-special brood
Of diplomat, but shortly gleaned
That one percent were good.

I never learned from Protocol
The right official tone;
I mostly found a French champagne
Superior to our own,
And felt that David Bruce made sense
In praising Gallic wines –
(I thought attacks on David read
Like comic valentines!)

I never learned to bend the knee
To bosses vain and dull
Who may have held a well-filled purse
But had an empty skull.
In fact, I never could abide
The State Department toff,
And so we went our separate ways –
Perhaps we're both well off!

Miscellaneous

A Gourmet's Creed

I love to dine with persons who
Are jolly, stout and rich,
Although they must be thick as glue
And suffering from the itch.

Why ask for mental somersaults
And intellectual cheer?
You get that from the library vaults –
You'll never find it here!

So why then feed with creatures who
Are sloppy, bright and thin,
Who dish up watered kidney stew
And have the neighbors in?

Provided that the bores be flush,
Let's skip the mental gains!
Provided that the girls be lush
Who cares about their brains?

A Southern Idyll

(as enacted after World War II)

The moon was a melon of silver, half hidden
By clusters of moss that hung down from the trees
And trailed on the neck of thoroughbred ridden
By Colonel Augustus Marcellus McSneeze.

He rode in the moonlight, a soldier of station,
Erect and as proud as the trees by his side,
Till he encountered the gates of the noble plantation
Of her whom he ardently wished for his bride.

He sprang from the saddle as strong as a lion;
He tethered his horse as so often before;
He curled his mustache; he loudly called "Bryan"
Until and old butler appeared at the door.

Then lifting his hat in an elegant manner
The Colonel inquired if Miss Maisie was home.
He pulled from his pocket a purple bandanna
And swabbed his perspiring and luminous dome.

He waited, scarce daring to breathe as he listened,
Till faintly there came a light step on the stair.
And holding his hand to a forehead that glistened,
He heard a sweet voice trill: "Gus? Are you there?"

"Oh, Maisie, my darling, I've tried hard to reach you."
He kissed her soft hand as he fell at her knees.
"Beloved, again I have come to beseech you
To marry Augustus Marcellus McSneeze!"

But sadly the maiden withdrew several paces
Despite his distress and his evident rage,
"Oh, dearest Augustus – you know –
It's your age."

"Must age," cried the soldier, his tears falling faster,
"With malice infernal our happiness freeze?
Shall time with its threats of impending disaster
Daunt Colonel Augustus Marcellus McSneeze?"

"Alas," sighed the girl, "as you say, it's infernal,
And living without you is bitter and drear,
But you're only 20, although you're a Colonel,
And Father insists that we wait for a year!"

ADVICE TO A CIGARETTE BUTT SMOKER

"A cigarette smoker wants to know which hand is correct for holding the butt."
...ESQUIRE

Dear Sir:

Even smokers experienced as you
May easily fall in a rut,
Hence, I feel it is nice to extend good advice
On the art of the cigarette butt.

A cigar, as you know, should be held with the thumb
And the fore-finger close to the nose—
Although scotch tape and gum are accepted by some,
And a pobble employs his toes.

A pipe—need I mention?—is always retained
In the hand holding biscuits and ale,
While the English insist on a flexible wrist,
And the leaf monkey uses his tail.

These pointers, of course, have appreciable force
In Queen Nicotine's new etiquette.
And there isn't a doubt you'll be often asked out
If you handle a smart cigarette.

I suggest that you shuffle your butts every day
In mahogany cigarette stands,
Then smoke each in turn till it ceases to burn
Using alternate elbows and hands.

Why not carry your butts in a humidor case
With a lid that is permanently shut?
Or start out in the Fall by not smoking at all?
I'm afraid I'm confusing you, but—

AGE

Age is the python's cast-off skin;
The frayed, discarded overcoat;
The trickle of reluctant gin
Down an old toper's scrawny throat.

Age is a grisly yellow fog
Through which soft-footed burglars creep
To where ten people and a dog
Lie unsuspectingly asleep.

Age is the quickly drying stain
Of tears that streaks the cynic's cheek;
Age is the twitch of nagging pain
That mars the acrobat's physique.

Age is all things to different men,
To some a curse, a malady;
To some a cage, a trap, a pen –
It's never meant a thing to me.

An Ambassador Apologizes to the Chief of Protocol

Dear Monsieur Chief de Protocol
Your name I quite forget,
Tho this does not affect at all
My sense of etiquette.

Last night I came Blair House down,
My lovely wife and I
She wore a stunning evening gown,
I wore my new black tie.

Our car drew up at Blair House gate,
Which gate was shut and barred.
I wondered: "Have we come too late?"
I found an empty yard.

No butler answered to my ring;
No footman to my knock.
Do Yankees dine at eight or nine,
Or maybe ten o'clock?

So home we went – no food to eat –
No dinner, wine or host.
Is this the way your friends you treat?
Is this of what you boast?

Today, your office gives a call.
The party is tonight!
Now, Monsieur Chief de Protocol,
This surely is not right.

With us it were a burning shame
Such liberties to take,
Inducing, Monsieur what's your name,
A diplomatic break.

However, an Ambassador
Should not at such slights swoon.
Forgive me that I come to dine
One little day too soon.

CALL OF THE WILD

I lie here like a wounded dog.
Around me nurses stand.
The doctor feels my pulse and shrugs,
Then drops my lifeless hand.

All over! Soon my soul must leave
This earth so warm and rich.
Just then rings out a vibrant shout:
"Get up, you son-of-a-bitch!"

Who spoke, who spoke those dreadful words
To call me from the tomb?
What spectre fled with lowered head
Out of my gin-soaked room?

I push the covers back. I rise.
You cannot hold me down.
Despite the doctor's clucks and cries
I dress and go to town.

I play. I dance; upon the turf
The horse-shoes gaily pitch.
I leap into the silver surf.
Get up, you son-of-a-bitch!

Get up, get up from bed or couch,
From coffin, grave or ditch!
Has Jesus said that you are dead?
Get up, you son-of-a-bitch!

Dear girl, whate'er my rare disease,
From stone to barber's itch,
Please, love, intone and never cease:
"Get up, you son-of-a-bitch!".

DREAM OF CHARLEMAGNE

When the ground is frozen and the dark leaves rustle,
And the silk is trimmed with fur on Grandmama's bustle;
When the cream is thinly iced, and the cat squalls,
And the leaping flames paint red dragons on the walls,
I breathe on the inside of the window pane
And dream about the days of the great Charlemagne.

Red gleams his curling beard – as red as the red dragons!
His corselet is Spanish steel; red wine swims in his flagons.
Spears shine with wet blood. Haggard and aloof,
Charlemagne rides a horse with a white hoof.

Violent bells thunder in a high steeple.
Bristling lines of warriors hold back the people –
Dark, merry people crowding to stare
At a pale lady with straggling hair.

Ring out, wild bells, on the callous air,
A paean to that pale head with the damp hair!
Bristle, spears, in a forbidding roof
To a red beard and a white hoof!

When the wind starts creeping and the sad leaves rustle,
And the silk is trimmed with fur on Grandmama's bustle;
When the crows are cawing over dead fields,
And the crazy candle a fitful radiance yields,
I pull up the covers like a ghostly train
And dream about the days of the great Charlemagne!

ELEGY IN A WOMAN'S DRESS SHOP AT 5:30 P.M.

The curfew tolls the knell of parting day,
The jabbering crowd winds up its buying spree;
The salesgirls homeward plod their weary way,
And leave this place to darkness and to me.

Now fades the glimmering tea-gown on the sight,
And all the air a solemn stillness holds,
Save where two straggling customers still fight
About the latest Valentina molds;

Save that from yonder many-mirrored booth
My lingering wife her theory reasserts,
That Paris stylist are absurd, forsooth,
And that she WILL NOT wear the longer skirts.

Behind these darkling panes, like treasure iced
In sunless splendor for a season's fad,
Each in its narrow berth discreetly priced,
Hang the creations that drive women mad.

Let not old Boredom mock the dresses here,
Their futile fate and destiny obscure,
Nor envy greet with resentful leer
The fancy doing of the "Haute Couture."

The boast of heraldry, the pomp of power,
And all that beauty, all that wealth e'er gave
May well await the inevitable hour –
But women's fashions keep ME from the grave!

Farewell to the Racing "Experts"

"LONDON, June 8 (AP) – Britain's racing 'experts' who guessed wrong – everyone – moaned in unison today and blamed everything from the weather to Gordon Richards's boots for the failure of an English-bred horse to win the turf event of the year, the Derby."

O sad is the dirge of the loud-sounding sea,
And sad are the cries of the loon;
Filled with horrid travail is the long banshee's wail
As it prowls 'neath the cold winter moon;
Most pitiful, too, are political moans
Of a party whose man cannot win –
But saddest of all is that heart-rending squall
For a horse that has failed to come in!

Where now is that promise of laurels and gold;
That smirk on the owner's smug face;
The trainer's wise leer, plus his hint in your ear
As the nag was led out for the race;
The jockey's pleased look, and that vast roar which shook
A mob standing tense on its toes?
Ah, where are those thrills and those hundred pound bills?
All vanished – all gone with the rose!

Baroda's proud prince has departed long since.
The race flags droop, wilted and wan.
With his head still unbowed, through the fast thinning crowd
Creeps the ghost of the old Aga Khan.
Why linger, ye experts unexpert in life:
Why stupidly chatter and write?
Far better to go, and dissembling your woe –
Fade quietly into the night!

FISHERMAN'S LUCK

I baited my hook with silver
And fished in the purple seas,
But all that I took from my silvery hook
Were some weeds like a green disease
And an anchor bound with a twisted round
Of lost sea-anemones.

I baited my hook with lipstick
And fished among sunken ships
Where I hoped to snatch from some rotting hatch
A mermaid with scaly hips.
What I found instead was a pale girl, dead,
With my lipstick clutched to her lips.

FLAMING YOUTH

Fell the night. From its nest in the deep velvet clover
A soft-throated nightingale sang.
I sighed: "Ah, at last all the day's noise is over!"
But uncle began his harangue.

"You send yellow roses to languorous creatures
Who swoon with delight in their tubs,
Who smear crimson lips on lascivious features
And revel in alcohol rubs!"

"Your beagling coats clutter the dining room table.
There's caviar fed to the cat.
You order silk stocking for women by cable –
Now, what is the use of all that?"

"Your measles and waistcoats alike are contagious.
You breakfast at half after four.
That bill for gold soup spoons was simply outrageous.
By God, I won't stand any more!"

Came the dawn. All the oriel windows were gleaming.
My uncle's beard sank to his breast.
I calmly set fire to his whiskers. His screaming
Deprived me of hours of rest.

FROM A PSYCHIATRIST'S CASE BOOK

(the man who had a compulsion to celebrate a noisy 4th of July)

As a child he was neither ferocious nor wild.
He was modest and terribly shy;
But he grew tense and wan at the first sign of dawn
On the glorious Fourth of July.

At the bright age of ten he succumbed to a yen
For burning up half of the town,
And he sat on his roof, quite reserved and aloof,
Until firemen escorted him down.

In a couple of years he was up to his ears
In lawsuits and beatings with canes.
If he hadn't been young he'd have surely been hung
For blowing up bridges and trains.

Neither Juvenile Court nor his pals managed aught
To repress this incredible guy
Who just couldn't wait for that memorable date –
The glorious Fourth of July.

For years he remained, as it were, self-contained,
And uttered no murmur of sound.
But a dawn's early streak he awoke with a shriek
When that glorious day rolled around.

With candle and wheel (plus unlimited zeal),
With fire-cracker, rocket and gun,
He would rage, scream and yell, waving banner and bell
At everything under the sun.

At last he was brought before Criminal Court
His various crimes to deny.
But the judge cried: "What nerve! Sure, no jail term you'll serve
On this glorious Fourth of July!"

GLOVED, SHE EATS TOAST

Teacups are clinking discreetly and gently.
Sleek in the snow outside glitters her Bentley.
Snug by the fire inside, Cynthia is purring.
Softly, so softly, her tea she keeps stirring.

Zippered and slippered and buttoned and belted,
Cold as an icicle love hasn't melted.
"Please, only one slice of lemon at most, pet!"
In her gloved hand she holds cinnamon toast, yet!

Purring and stirring, with eyes of a panther,
Brimming with schemes as a wood flower's anther,
Brimful with pollen, wise as a siren,
Soft as a kitten and harder than iron.

GRANDFATHER'S JEST

Grandfather spoke. His voice was rich and able.
"My darling child, perhaps I needn't mention
That I have kicked you twice beneath the table
To draw your eyes and focus your attention."

"Pass me that bottle! Never mind the cat –
It's had its dinner! Light me a cigar!
Good!... Fetch my Swedish muffler and my hat
And tell the man to bring around the car!"

He combed his beard with many a pleasing wrinkle,
His diamonds glittered feebly in the gloom.
His starched dress shirt went softly "crinkle, crinkle."
He looked like one who dresses for the tomb.

That night he had an extra cup of coffee,
Also a fainting spell at half-past two.
The doctor called. Grandfather said: "Keep off me!"
The doctor said: "Whom are you talking to?"

"Your years and sardine fisheries have made you callous.
A man of ninety-eight should be polite.
Only good luck has saved you from the gallows
To let you die beneath my axe tonight."

The crisis passed; the invalid grew better
And promptly changed his medicines for wines.
The doctor wrote a most insulting letter –
Grandfather sent him comic valentines.

HEREDITY

Sir Oswald Ryecroft Bingwell-James
Was very fond of ancient games--
Old-fashioned, quiet, mild affairs,
The kind one plays in easy-chairs.
On rainy days he tried besique,
Besides parcheesi twice a week
With gouty colonels who adored
The thrill of a parcheesi board.
So when his niece, Amanda Brink,
Who lived in Upper Bobolink,
Asked to come spend a month with him,
He was delighted by her whim.
"I don't," he wrote her, "favor dice,
But ecarte is very nice –
Or we'll play ombre which , as you know,
Was played two centuries ago."

So hoping that his niece inclined
To pasttimes simple and refined,
Sir Oswald went and bought champagne
And hurried down to meet the train.
He didn't know exactly how
Amanda looked. He thought by now
She must be fairly old and frail.
He'd stored away some gingerale
In case they frowned on stronger drink
In holes like Upper Bobolink.

The train arrived. Sir Oswald grinned
At an old lady, double-chinned
And plump and pink, with a great brooch
Of jet, who tottered from the coach.
"Amanda dear," he sighed and took
Her worn valise and hymnal book.
"How well you look, my dearest niece!"

The dear old lady screamed "Police!"
"But are you not Amanda Brink,
My niece from Upper Bobolink?"
The dear old lady shook her head.
"I'm Mrs. Appleby," she said.
"I'm 83. I live in Kew
And disapprove of tramps like you.
Who molest honest working girls.
Be off!" She shook her snowy curls
And grabbed her bag and book, and fled
To safety in the station shed.

Sir Oswald, dazed, just stood and stared,
When suddenly a voice blared:
"Hi, Uncle!" and – O Gracious God! –
There was his niece, a dreadful clod!
She wore a kind of tweedy coat
That stank of country cheese and goat.
Her face was red, her bosom wide,
She carried golf clubs by her side,
Three tennis racquets and a pack
Of rods and reels and fishing tack.
With sinking heart, Sir Oswald smiled.
"Welcome!" said he, "My dearest child!"
Then, as he kissed her on the chin,
He caught a whiff of Gordon's gin.

At home, though plunged in heavy gloom,
He showed her gaily to her room.
"We dine at 8," he bowed. "Perhaps ...
Before our meal... a touch of Schnapps?"
"Schnapps!" sneered his niece. "Hell! Count me out!"
I'll have a whiskey, Unc – or stout.
And after dinner, what's the plan?
Maybe we'll need an extra man!"
She dug him in the ribs and leered.
The case seemed worse than he had feared.

Groaning, he ran downstairs to play
At patience. Would she go away?
He doubted it. In sudden fear
He wondered if she'd stay a year.

The weeks slipped by. Amanda Brink
From no atrocity did shrink.
Despite her uncle's mild retorts
She laughed to scorn his indoor sports.
She left the windows open wide
To let "God's good clear air" inside.
Mosquitos, too! She'd merely shrug.
"Christ, Uncle! What's a little bug?"
She swam, she rode, she scored at golf.
She kicked her uncle's poodle, "Rolf";
She drank, caroused, came home at five.
The wretched Oswald, half alive,
Dragged at her heels. He moaned "A souse!
Oh, what a curse upon the house!"
He cancelled dates with startled friends;
He felt that zest which evil lends
When once he horrified the vicar
Who found him overcome with liquor.

Yet strange! The more that Oswald drank
And drew his money from the bank
To finance games she had refused
To play, the less his niece enthused
The more he read the sporting journals,
The more she patronized the colonels
Who – one by one – crept back to play
Their quiet round of ecarté
And ombre and dominoes and such.
They grew accustomed to her, much
As deer penned in a private park
Grow callous to the deer-hound's bark.
By stages gradual and easy

Amanda got to like parcheesi,
And on one fateful afternoon
She played with Colonel Witherspoon.

Swift was her fall! The following week
She took up cribbage and besique
While old Sir Oswald, rather fried,
Set up the bowling pins outside.
There hardly came a day or night
When he was not absurdly tight.
No longer did he care to stress
The vast advantages of chess
As against rugby or affirm
That every athlete was a worm.
A fiend on tennis, golf and racing,
He spent his evenings woman-chasing
And guzzling every sort of drink
To the distress of poor Miss Brink
Who, in her atmosphere bucolic,
Was now a fierce non-alcoholic.

Comes quick the ending of the tale.
Sir Oswald's health began to fail.
Too many drinks, too much excitement –
A late and merry life's indictment –
Brought the result one might expect.
His grave with many wreaths was decked
From friends who in an older day
Had played with him at ecarte.
Not least, from sweet Amanda Brink,
Lately of Upper Bobolink,
Came a huge cross of honeysuckle
Marked (they forgot the "N") "DEAR UCKLE."
Now, like Sir Oswald, every week
Amanda plays a mean besique
Although they say that her canasta
Is an incredible disaster

And she has not yet dared to dabble
In anything as rash as scrabble!

How To Spoil a Husband

You rouse him in the morning with an eardrum piercing yell;
You lead him to a mirror and declare he looks like hell;
You burn the toasted muffins and exclaim: "It's getting late"
When he tries to sneak a second piece of bacon on his plate.

You hide the maple syrup: "Dear, you're getting much too fat;"
You praise the sexual prowess of a local acrobat;
You twist the TV needle to "New Fashions by Priscilla"
Although he'd rather listen to some corny Western thriller.

If he puffs a fine Havana you discreetly pinch your nose;
When he wants a touch of quiet you recount domestic woes;
Perhaps he's feeling poorly and would like to laze or shirk –
Well, just remind him sharply that it's time to go to work!

———————

At last the funeral's over! You've left the burial ground;
You've had your third Martini as the neighbors gather 'round.
Then, o'er the sound of sobbing and the conversation's buzz,
You tell his aunt and sister what a lovely guy he was!

IDLENESS

She sat and gazed at the drifting snow,
And nibbled an onyx pen.
She said: "I'll write him that letter now
Which I owe since God knows when."

She rubbed her lips with a stick of red.
She mirrored her shining teeth.
She wondered, "Should I re-do my bed
With a pot-de-chambre underneath?"

She mused on the thought of Valenciennes
Draped over an Empire couch.
She swatted a fly with "Vie Parisienne"
And distractedly muttered "ouch!"

The sun went down in a purple haze.
She went to a boring dinner.
She dieted for a couple of days
And found she was getting thinner.

She attended a lecture long and dull,
And wept for the Ethiopian.
She thought that the views of Cordell Hull
Were liberal-but Utopian.

An evening fell when the frosted loam
Reflected a soft, sad light.
She combed her hair with a silver comb
And sighed: "I'll write him tonight."

INTERLUDE AT TIVOLI

To always wait is man's estate, and this I've always done.
(In Protocol one waits for years and tries to call it fun.)
I wait in dismal drawing rooms for Princes to arise;
I wait for planes, for taxis, trains – for all that runs or flies.

I've waited at the Eagle in the Wanamaker store,
'Cause "Meet me at the Eagle!" was a rendezvous of yore;
I've yearned to hear the postman's knock and harkened for the squeak
Of garden gates which meant the note I'd hungered for all week.

I've stood by purring limousines and clutched an opera hat
Awaiting the departure of some boring diplomat;
I've waited to identify a body at the morgue;
I waited once for Denmark's Queen outside Amalienborg.

But what is worse than lying in pajamas on your bed
And wrestling pillows, waiting for the girl you want instead?
You writhe, you snarl, you stretch, you hope, you pray, you groan, you twist,
You turn from scanning etchings to the new Best Seller list.

You have her whispered promise, so your door is on the latch;
The light's discreetly lowered and you've drawn the curtains, natch!
But now it's after midnight... You're feeling sick and glum,
You know... you know for certain, that she isn't going to come!

Last Call

"Last call!" The voice rang sharply out.
The pullman porter glanced about
As if offering champagne and caviar.
"Last call for dinner in the dining car!"

"Last call!" The diners walked briskly back.
How could they know of a cow on the track?
Do we ever know what our futures are?
"Last call for dinner in the dining car!"

"Last call!" – Suddenly lurched the train...
A crash!... An angel took up the refrain,
Counting the dead by the light of a star:
"Last call for sinners in the dining car!"

NOSTALGIA FOR SHANGRI-LA

I'm sick of the worry and scurry of life –
If you haven't a cold, then you fight with your wife,
Or your brother has rabies, your cousin's in town,
Your mistress wants babies or a new evening gown.
I'm tired of the noise of neighbors and cats,
And warm cocktails served in impossible flats
By loud, stupid persons incredibly rich –
(You can bet that your host is a son-of-a-bitch!)
I'm bored by long speeches of ponderous men,
And dinners that start at a quarter to ten,
And women who, married, still go out on dates,
Then confide the details to their credulous mates.

I'm fed up with Frenchmen and fairies and Finns,
And ladies with poodles and three double chins,
And phone calls from persons named Gumbulch or Zkeek
Requesting my presence at breakfast next week,
And rent bills and dentists and horrible scenes
With waiters, neurotics and ex-movie queens.
It's awful to think how we're breaking our necks
To get just the merest sensation of sex.
Why <u>should</u> one show etchings and pour out one's heart
To vapid young things who know nothing of art?
Why pay for martinis and music and wine
To make poor meandering Millicent mine?

I want to go places where sex crawls around
With stomach and breast-bone pressed close to the ground –
Not swishing about trailing sashes and fur,
And as sad as a dog done by Rosa Bonheur.
I crave tropic isles where the girls wear no clothes
And the Chief goes around with a ring in his nose;
Where the sands are like silver, the sea is like silk,
And you lie on your back and drink coconut milk;

Where the palms softly sway in the languorous breeze,
And the only sound heard is the jaguar's sneeze,
And monkeys go mad simply picking their ears,
And a sailing ship calls every couple of years.

Yea, give me the tropics! 'Tis there I would go,
Where life is unbearably, terribly slow.
'Tis there – in a tent of rhinoceros hide –
That I... oh, at least for a month... would abide!

PICK-UP IN GREECE

The wave crashed on the Aegean shore
And out of the fragments stepped a fish whose face
Would have driven Alcibiades crazy
And that Socrates would have termed a
Disgrace.

It strolled across and sat beneath the sun-shade
Of the girl in the new Dior gown,
Lifting a fin politely and bowing slightly,
While carefully looking her up
And down.

"Excuse me, dear, but do you speak Hindustani,
Greek, Urdu, French, Italian, or Czech?"
"No, I don't even speak English, Jack." said the maiden,
And she gave the fish a whack that broke
Its neck.

ON THE EFFECT OF VARIOUS DRINKS

When I drink whiskey, as I often do,
I wonder what this world's coming to
And about soul yearnings and Standard Oil
And why men sweat and suffer and toil.

When I drink gin (if there's nothing better)
I talk to a girl – though I haven't met her –
About Greece and Plato, which is quite ironic
Because I don't feel the least platonic.

When I drink champagne I bubble over
And pat little dogs and call them "Rover"
And offer old ladies another cup,
And everyone says: "Oh, God! Shut up!"

When I drink sweet rum or a brandy punch
I seldom arrive in time for lunch;
My speech grows strangely, suddenly thick
And soon I get disgustingly sick!

ON THE LAUDABLE PHILOPSOPHY OF SELF-IMPROVEMENT

There were two tribes of God-forsaken natives.
One tribe read Greek and conjugated datives;
The other was so frankly un-Bostonian
It actually had eaten an Etonian.
One day, an anthropologist who studied features
Came out to write an essay on these creatures.
The tribe that specialized in mental bunions
Spared him because it thought he smelled of onions.
The cultured tribe, whose chief had been to college,
Devoured him, that it might digest his knowledge.

QUESTION MARK

Will you kindly explain the reason why
So many charming people die,
While all around – in bars, in ditches –
The world is full of sons-of-bitches?

They tag your car, they steal your shirt,
They peddle the dirtiest kind of dirt.
They lie, they cheat, they pile up wealth
And all enjoy amazing health.

Yet every day (just read the press!)
There's at least one delightful creature less.
Some girl you knew with violet eyes,
Exquisite, lovely – ups and dies.

Some worthwhile, honest, steady friend
With seven children, meets his end...
A bug, a germ, a hacking cough,
A heart condition takes them off.

But all around – just count them, brother!
The sons-of-bitches kiss each other.
No pain. No woe. No jittery drunks.
Hell, no! They're happy being skunks.

Quite frankly, logic makes me wonder
If being charming is not a blunder.
Maybe the best way to dodge a wreath
Is to kick nice people in the teeth!

ON THE SUPERIORITY OF THE IMPRACTICAL MIND

Having a quiet business chat,
A butter salesman and a poet
High up on Mt. Olympus sat
And gazed upon the plains below it.

"A gorgeous spot," the poet cooed.
"I think great thoughts I dare not utter."
Far down the vale a stray cow mooed.
"I think," the salesman said, "of butter."

"Ah, yes!" The poet gave a sigh.
"This altitude brings on a dizziness.
Let's see! You get my books – and I
Acquire an interest in your business."

The salesman crowed, "My offer stands.
These thousand drachmas here will show it."
He shoved them in the other's hands.
"Butter and butter!" cried the poet.

"Gaze down! Behold, O man of doubt,
A view of beauty unalloyed."
Then, as the salesman leaned far out,
He pushed him neatly through the void.

———————

In Athens now, with well-filled purse,
The poet writes – though critics mutter –
His lovely Alexandrine verse
Exclusively on pats of butter.

PORTRAIT OF A KING

You must not serve him
Bordeaux wines nor sherry
with the shad –
You must not cross your
legs, because shoe leather
drives him mad.
His Majesty likes any food for
breakfast, tea or lunch –
But you may slip a sheep's
eye in his evening orange punch.

His Majesty likes comfort, and
sends scoundrels to their doom
By signing all death warrants
in an air-conditioned room –
And annually he undertakes
The pilgrimage to Mecca
Relaxing on the cushions of
a scarlet double-decker.

His dagger laced with diamonds
and his agals black and gold,
Enhance a regal aspect
rather fearful to behold
Though he suffers from lumbago and
a touch of nerve sciatic,
Plus all the usual ailments –
that afflict an Asiatic.

An ardent "Life" subscriber, he
wires New York collect
when he gives his standing order
in an Arab dialect.

He gets his latest copy,
not delivered camel-back
But by a sheik who brings it
in a brand-new Cadillac.

All Hail our famous visitor!
Of royalty we sing
His country's soil holds tons of oil –
All hail, All hail the King!

THE CHANGING FACE OF BEAUTY

I took a beautiful hungry girl
To lunch beside the river.
A bright but unseen Cupid drew
An arrow from his quiver.

He aimed the arrow at our hearts.
It might have caused a flutter
Had not my hungry girl mistook
Her lipstick for the butter!

SEASIDE ROMANCE

I met her quite casually
At the Lido beach.
Eyes of lapis lazuli;
Skin of pearl and peach;

Silver-blue bikini –
Very nice to see.
We had had a Martini,
Maybe two or three.

Name of Mariandl;
Lovely, slightly wild.
Shouldn't cause a scandal
Just to kiss the child.

Ice and inhibitions
Melting in the sun.
Little coy admissions;
Hearts that beat as one.

Man comes looking haggard,
Jealous eyes aglow.
Oh, it seems she's married!
Oh, I didn't know!

Name of Sherbatuvksy;
Very pleased to meet.
Polish, big and husky.
Boy, be discreet!

Eyes of lapis lazuli
Turn to eyes of jet.
I left her as casually
As we two had met.

TALE OF THE SOUSE

There lived a guy whose mild blue eye
Was guileless if demented;
Who filled his skin with scotch and gin,
Quite happy and contented.

His liquid feast disturbed no beast,
His eye rebuked no sinner;
Whene'er he'd scan a fellow-man
He'd ask him home to dinner.

A modest plat of whiskey straight,
Soon followed by a bracer;
Then to delight the appetite
More whiskey as a chaser.

He thrived for years on gin and beers,
A charming, witty fellow
Whose only fault was mixing malt
And growing somewhat mellow.

Then to his den in Drunkards' Glen
Came persons to confound him
With cataracts of fancy tracts,
To badger and impound him.

They choked his screams with chocolate creams
And fed him eggs and bacon
Which they declared had been prepared
His moral sense to waken.

Within a week his poor physique
At death's door lay reclining,
They brought a quill and cried: "Your will!
Your will you must be signing!"

But while the mob with sigh and sob
Imagined he was sinking,
He bravely scrawled an opus called:
"The Benefits of Drinking."

"NEW YORK, September 11 (AP) –
Bishop Homer A. Tomlinson of the Church of God said today he would sue his brother, Bishop Milton A. Tomlinson, for recovery of their father's diary and $5,000,000 damages. The diary of the late Bishop A.J. Tomlinson has been the subject of a four-year controversy between the two brothers."

When Bishop A.J. Tomlinson
Was blessed with two small sons,
He vowed they'd be a credit to
The line of Tomlinsons;
And since he was a cleric of
Much scholarly repute,
He sought to give them names remote
From biblical dispute.

He thumbed his classic history
And found a fitting text.
So one lad's name spelled Grecian fame,
And English lore the next.
Who would have thought to view them in
Their cradles, pink and cute,
That Homer would sue Milton in
A brotherly dispute?

Wise Bishop A.J. Tomlinson
In course of nature died.
To Milton went his diary;
To Homer went his pride;
While, to the lawyers soon must go
The profits of the suit,
Which Homer slapped on Milton in
A brotherly dispute.

Whether Dad's diary is his goal
The item fails to say.
If Homer wins it, will he toss
Five million bucks away?
We do not know, yet must suspect,
Though evidence be mute,
That money counts for something in
This brotherly dispute.

And so, to Bishops Tomlinson,
Yea, Milt and Homer both!
A hint about the Needle's Eye, the camel and their oath.
What difference 'twixt the priestly jowl
And countenance hirsute,
If bishops take to suing in
A brotherly dispute?

Proud princes may sue garbage men,
And kittens may sue kings,
And columnists sue daily in
The general run of things,
But sad it is for morals and
For manner dissolute
When a bishop sues his brother in
A brotherly dispute!

THE DERVISH WHO STOPPED WHIRLING – TEMPORARILY

It happened in Benares, that city sad and quaint
Where the dervish in his kaftan is regarded as a saint;
Where the inter-turban traffic is exceptionally brisk
And the vulture is considered as a good insurance risk.

Old Abou Mahmoud Hassan, combing splinters from his beard,
Was of all the whirling dervishes especially revered.
He whirled from dawn to sunset; he whirled while others sleep.
He whirled when younger dervishes were howling in a heap.

But whirls like all good things must end, and old Ben Abou's whirl
Was ended by romance with the Rajah's dancing girl.
The Rajah slapped the lipstick from the erring Ziska's lips
And put her friend the whirler into temporary eclipse.

Then, in the second moon or third, one evening very late,
While Abou Mahmoud Hassan sat reflecting on his fate,
A sudden key-lock grated and through the moonlit gloom
He saw Ziska – lovely Ziska – come spinning in the room.

"O Lover, in the market place the vultures bill and coo
As if waiting for a banquet and I'm fearful it is you!
Come, let us fly to Europe! I have sold the Rajah's pearl."
Old Abou donned his afghan and retorted: "Let us whirl!"

Terrific was the whirling in Benares on the day
When the Rajah found that Abou and his girl had whirled away.
The inter-turban traffic made harmonious accord
With the whirling of the vultures and the headman's gleaming sword.

But Abou Mahmoud Hassan, I am happy to confess,
Was whirling to the rhythm of the Delhi-Rome Express!

THE HERMIT WHO CAME IN FROM THE COLD

The hermit mused on long-lost loves
All cooked his frugal dinner...
Eileen had fancied white kid gloves,
Yvonne had backed a winner;
It was Nell's habit
To toast Welsh rarebit!

Across his dream the bloodhounds bayed,
A gorgeous girl came riding.
"O ancient imbecile," she said.
"Why spend your life in hiding?
Have you God's permit
To be a hermit?"

She combed the splinters from his beard,
His savage air extinguished
With a shampoo, and he appeared
Disgustingly distinguished.
"You needed fixin',"
Explained the vixen.

With brilliantine she smoothed his hair,
Gave him a shot of Bourbon;
Then dragged him from his mountain lair
Into a site suburban.
Soon all the papers
Laughed at his capers.

Thus did a witch with sexy eyes
Seduce a saintly hermit,
This she-wolf wore a "sheep's disguise,"
As mid-Victorians term it.
It was her fashion
To play with passion.

THE MAN WHO WAS ALWAYS FALLING

He first fell from his crib
And fractured half a rib —
(He was reaching for a little toy rabbit!) —
Then, as a general rule,
He fell each week at school
'Till very soon the thing became a habit.

He broke his wrist and nose;
He dislocated toes—
(They bought him artificial toes from Bendix!) —
And on one slippery day
Some ice got in his way —
He fell again and ruptured his appendix.

Five doctors sent him pills,
Plus the most outrageous bills;
They patched his arms, they taped his legs and tummy.
Ensconced in straps and strands,
Entwined with crisscross bands,
He looked like an obscene Egyptian mummy.

At last this dreadful wreck
Fell down and broke his neck —
(The undertaker slipped and dropped the coffin!) —
And at St. Peter's gate
They asked him please to wait —
Even his soul had fallen once too often!

THE MAN WHO WAS NEVER LATE — WELL, HARDLY EVER!

The clock struck nine. The chief looked up
And growled in low but fervent tones:
"Take down a memo, Buttercup.....
Say, where the hell is Oswald Jones?"

"He's never late. For twenty years
His key has grated in the lock
Each morning – or, so it appears –
Upon the stroke of eight o'clock!"

Then, with averted, tear-dimmed eyes
A boy approached the chief and said:
"Poor Mr. Jones in heaven flies!
There is no doubt that he is dead."

"His black bow-tie, his topaz ring,
His elk tooth on the silver chain,
That dreadful suit he bought last Spring –
We shall not see these things again."

"We shall not hear the timid cough
With which he touched you for a loan –
His debt is paid. All bets are off.
He walks before God's golden throne."

"A harp of gold is in his hand
Instead of poker chips and dice.
Two seraph angels by him stand
And serve him ginger ale and ice."

But LO! A clamor drowned their grief,
And loud the office staff did cuss,
As Jones, defiant, faced the chief:
"I <u>know</u> I'm late. I missed my bus!"

THE MINT-JULEP PARTY

Judge Ambler, in a flowered vest,
Sat chatting with a favored guest,
Old Colonel Cramp of Hollow Oak,
Who'd driven over for a smoke.
Upon the terrace broad and wide
They gazed across the countryside
Through julep glasses. At their feet,
Fat from excess of bones and meat –
Exhausted by his master's bounty –
Lay Gredig, worst dog in the county.

The juleps passed. An hour slipped by...
They talked of cotton crops and why
Judge Ambler's son should head both tickets
For sheriff and jail those goddamn pickets.
They spoke of taxes and the fire
At Widow Hawkins and the buyer
Of thoroughbreds who'd gone up North.
The talk rolled gently back and forth.
Judge Ambler called: "More juleps, Sam!"
He peered into his glass. "God damn!
"A God damn moth has fallen in!"
He wiped the whiskey from his chin,
Then poked around among the ice.
"More juleps, Sam! I've asked you twice!"
The juleps passed... A silver husk
Of moon gleamed faintly through the dusk.

"Pray have you heard of the caprice
"Which caused my 18-year-old niece
"To shoot herself?" Judge Ambler said.
"I didn't know that she was dead."
Said Colonel Cramp. He looked surprised
Yet somewhat pleased for he surmised

That niece might be the one who'd stoned
Last year the Stropshire bull he owned.

"She's dead." Judge Ambler made reply.
"In fact, quite dead since last July.
"Great pity, that!" The learned Judge
Looked at a fly but did not budge
When the same fly crawled down his nose
And perched there, splendid in repose.

The juleps passed. The frosty mint
Shone like some rare old aquatint
Of luscious green. "You did not know
"My sister's child, Sapolio?
"A lovely creature, tall and fair,
"With dark grey eyes and long damp hair."

"Now, wait a bit," said Colonel Cramp.
"Do tell me why her hair was damp!"
Judge Ambler sadly shook his head.
"She bathed continually," he said.
"Continually?"... "Yes, night and day.
"We could not keep that girl away
"From bathtubs... Yes, a perfect scamp!
"And – well, that's why her hair was damp."

The juleps passed. A firefly rose
From the magnolia tree. "A pose,"
Judge Ambler said, "of modern youth.
"Baths! Stuff and nonsense! Tell the truth
"And shame the devil! Take my Maw —
"She's never even broke the law.
"At church each Sunday... feeds the sick...
"She raised me with a hickory stick...
"A model mother... perfect wife...
"And not one bath in all her life!"
Judge Ambler paused. "Since I was wed
"I ain't had one myself," he said.

"But what about your niece?" asked Cramp.
"A suicide, you say?... "A vamp!
"A siren, sir! A Circe! Fudge!
"I have no patience," cried the Judge,
"With girls who go and have a kid,
"Unmarried... Well that's what she did."
"You mean?" The Colonel's voice was low.
"THAT happened to Sapolio?"
"It did." A silence fell. One heard
The trilling of a mockingbird
Somewhere. The Judge resumed his tale:

"She shot herself. Some worthless male
"Got her in trouble. Don't know who.
"Might be the sheriff – might be you."
The Colonel spoke out loud and cold:
"Judge Ambler, you are growing old.
"Your memory's poor. I recollect
"Some things that most folks just suspect.
"Remember back in '92
"Those days – those times with Mary Lou?
"Be careful, friend! Just watch your tongue.
"Some folks live long and some – get hung."

Judge Ambler stood. His flowered vest
Rippled and wrinkled on his chest.
"Blackmail?" he said. "I'll handle that."
One hand grabbed Colonel Cramp's cravat.
His other seized the julep glass
Bordered with silver... made a pass...
CRASH! Like an oak tree Cramp fell down,
Blood on his forehead. With a frown,
Stupidly staring, stood the Judge.
Then, with his old expression: "Fudge!
"Yes, double fudge!" he cried. "You swine!
"You've had your girls and I've had mine.

"But don't your ever dare to snitch
"On me, you dirty son-of-a-bitch!"

The Colonel groaned and flicked an eye.
"Oh, God! My head," he moaned. "Oh, my!"
He lay relaxed a little space.
The dog walked over and licked his face
As who should say: "Look here, old pal,
Why all this fuss about a gal?"
Then presently, in a stupor still,
Old Cramp stood up and said: "I'm ill."
Judge Ambler answered not at all.
Half-dazed, he leaned against the wall
And once he muttered: "God damn tramp!
"And – well, that's why her hair was damp!"

"Goodbye!" the Colonel said, polite
Though bleeding. "Ambler! Hey! Goodnight!
"Oh, Christ, but I feel awfully sick!"
He gave poor Gredig's rump a kick.
"You lousy dog! I'll run along
"Oh, God, Judge! Weren't those juleps strong?"

THE NEPHEW WHO DISAPPEARED

He loved those darkened luncheon dens
With zebra skins and borscht,
So dim the waiter guided him
With an electric torch.

He reveled in the ghostly gloom
Of each exotic haunt.
And, stumbling through the murk, he'd cry:
"A perfect restaurant!"

One day he took his maiden aunt
Into so black a coop
That patrons, groping for their food,
Strewed glow-worms in their soup.

Aunt Mildred, terrified, reached out
To touch her newphew's coat,
But found that she was holding hands
With some old, whiskered goat.

"Oh, Harold! Harold!" screamed his aunt.
She screamed for him in vain,
For he had vanished in the dark
And was not seen again.

The Sad Fate of Blandish McWhite

O ye who the fierce-biting rays of the sun
In their terrible splendor would woo,
Beware of the plight of poor Blandish McWhite!
The same thing could happen to you.

Young Blandish McWhite journeyed down from the North
The hot Southern sun for to seek.
A well-spoken lad who unfortunately had
A delicate, pallid physique.

He rushed to the beach in the sheerest of shorts,
Affronting the glare and the heat.
Inhibitions released, like a strip tease artiste,
Affording the gallery a treat.

"O Blandish!" his friends cried in tones of distress,
"Beware of that old devil sun!"
But, ignoring their grief and grammatically brief,
He retorted: "It don't hurt me none."

With his attitude bland, Bland relaxed in the sand.
He gloriously sizzled and fried.
To a stranger who said: "Are you right in the head?"
"It don't hurt me none," he replied.

From a pink to a mauve, then a lavender hue,
His body grew richer in shade.
When the sun as of old sank in the crimson and gold
McWhite the same colors displayed.

That night on the beach a lone coast guard patrol
Some smoldering embers effaced.
As he wandered on by, he observed with a sigh:
"Them picknickers sure leave a waste!"

THE SEDUCTION OF LADY GROUSE

On rare occasions Lady Grouse,
Daughter of old Lord Wavertree,
Had been invited by a friend
To come and summer by the sea.

The friend, we may as well avow,
Was known in certain circles as
A "fille de joie" who years ago
Had walked the pavements of La Paz.

Married to a Bolivian rake,
She had reformed, grown fat and rich,
And was by her divorced Don Juan
Referred to as "that precious bitch."

One April when the lilac bloomed
And Lady Grouse was having tea
A careless servant dropped a pot
Of marmalade on Lord Wavertree.

Physicians came. Some said "Too bad!"
Some said "concussion of the brain."
Some said "pneumonia." Anyhow,
His Lordship died in frightful pain.

His will was read. O dreadful day!
This jewel of aristocrats
Had left his fortune to endow
A London hospital for cats.

Quite disillusioned, Lady Grouse,
So languid, languorous and frail,
Started in bleak despair to drink
A glass of cyanide and ale.

But since it only made her ill
(Though frail, she was a hardy wench)

They used a pump and let her go
After a lecture from the bench.

'Twas then that lovely Lady Grouse
Decided to go down and be
A guest for several days, at least,
Of Mrs. Sanchez by the sea.

An envelope of violet hue
Embossed with lions belching fire
Announced that Lady Grouse would come
On Thursday next to "Heart's Desire."

Some lingering sentiment perhaps,
From Buenos Aires or Buffalo
Had caused the aging prostitute
To name her Devon mansion so.

Thursday arrived. The hostess cooed:
"Welcome to 'Heart's Desire,' my dear!
Now, go and rest. We dine at nine.
Thomas will wake you, never fear."

Up the long stair of "Heart's Desire,"
Preceded by the footman's tread,
Walked Lady Grouse reflecting that
She must undress and go to bed.

And thus reflecting raised her head
And in the mirror at her side
She caught a glimpse of Thomas, tall,
Slender, sedate and dignified.

She liked his lips, his eyes, his hips,
The way he wore the Sanchez crest.
They reached her room, he left. She sighed
And, thinking of Thomas still, undressed.

She touched her breasts in thoughtful vein
She wrapped her body in a towel.

She heard outside the window-pane
The vagrant hooting of an owl...

Darkness and owls and distant waves
Beating upon the Devon shore...
She wondered wildly; Is this love?
And who is knocking at my door?

One knock! Two knocks! "Milady, please!"
He fumbled quickly for the light.
It flashed, and there stood Lady Grouse,
Clutching a towel, pale with fright.
"The owls! They scare me Thomas!"
In the somewhat thrilling interlude
She felt a hand creep 'round her thigh
And realized that she was nude...

———————

On rare occasions Lady Grouse,
Daughter of old Lord Wavertree,
Is still invited by her friend
To come and summer by the sea.

The waves beat ever on the shore;
The owls as always hoot and wail.
Old Mrs. Sanchez croons and broods.
But Thomas – that's another tale.

Lord Wavertree, it seems, had left
A second will around the house;
She got the money, after all,
So Thomas now serves Lady Grouse!

THE SIMPLE LIFE

Lord Abercomby Water-Cress
Owned an estate at Inverness.
It boasted 20,000 acres
And had been purchased from some Quakers
Who, in the days of Charles the Second,
Its value as a hide-out reckoned.
The mansion, tall and castellated,
Was most felicitously rated
As, next to Windsor, quite the tops
In architectural lollipops.
Each visitor admired its towers;
Its bathrooms with their glass-in showers;
Its hall adorned with coats of arms;
Its modern, burglar-proof alarms;
Its tapestries and ancient clocks;
Its dungeons sealed with mighty locks;
Its moat, its turrets and its drain
Designed to fill the tubs with rain.

About it velvet countryside
All glossy smooth, stretched far and wide,
Dotted with sheep and Guernsey cows
Which on the greenery would browse
With just the air one should possess
If browsing for Lord Water-Cress.
On pleasant summer afternoons
His lordship's friends with silver spoons
Fed the proud swans that glided o'er
The pond beyond the purple moor,
Or hailed the furtive, timid deer
That eyed them with a look of fear.
Beneath the elms, alive with rooks,
Were mossy, partly hidden nooks

Where in the autumn one might rest
On marble benches to digest
The ptarmigan and golden grouse
Served – on hot platters – from the house
By footmen – twenty men at most –
Dressed in the livery of the host.

These bright, informal, gay affairs –
Where guests in flannels strolled in pairs
About the grounds, were greated liked –
Especially when the punch was spiked.
"How charming is Lord Water-Cress,"
They'd sigh. "How lovely Inverness!
Ah, here one finds normality
Devoid of all formality.
No stuffy, dull, imposing group –
No Spanish olives with the soup –
No pomp – one lackey to each guest...
Ah, what a place to come to rest!"
Thus conversation lightly flowed
As in this rustic, plain abode
Chefs and their helpers clothed in white
Concocted, to the guests' delight,
Such gems of culinary art
As might have warmed Escoffier's heart;
Meanwhile – with a true gourmet's tact –
The big wine cellars were ransacked
For precious wines whose mere aroma
Sent connoisseurs in a coma.
The kitchen-maids were in a tizzy;
The telephones were always busy
As servants called for extra fare –
Sovrani's furnished roasted bear;
Ten cases of a favorite wine
Were ordered from the Argentine;
Fresh game from Africa 'd arrive

Crated and luscious, still alive,
And once – from the Grand Duchess Olga
They sent for sturgeon from the Volga.

This simple and unspoiled dream
Of country life, made London seem
So ponderous and still and formal
That to reside there seemed abnormal.
So, gradually each relative
Or Abercromby came to live
At Inverness where care unfurled
Her worries and forgot the world –
The stinking, filthy omnibus;
The shouting, clamor, stir and fuss;
The nightclub and the dank café;
The dust, the dreadful business day;
The luxury, the over-dressed,
Grand, boring people and the rest.
No wonder that to get away
His Lordship's nieces came to stay;
His aunts, his uncles and his brothers;
Some maiden cousins and their mothers –
A brother-in-law who sent a wire
From a small town in Devonshire.

All came to Inverness prepared
To greet His Lordship, who declare:
"Formality I'll always hate.
It is a menace to the state.
You see, we live the simple life.
No protocol down here is rife.
Arcadian simplicity,
Dear cousins, is enough for me.
Aside from my small retinue
Wearing the ducal 'W' –
The butlers, footmen, pages, grooms,
The maids, of course, who clean the rooms –

The gardeners, chefs and extra cooks –
The man who dusts my library books –
The man who winds the clocks each Monday –
The special staff that works on Sunday –
My valet, my Scotland Yard detective –
His work is really quite effective –
Aside from these, my secretary
Whom I regard as necessary
(His name is Anastasius Wimple)
My life, dear friends is <u>very simple</u>.
No luxury, no etiquette!
I have a horror of the set
And stupid, useless grandeur which
Alas – surround the very rich –
But come – let's go and view the lawns
Or take some cake and feed the swans."

Then this enchanting, simple peer –
Escorted by a brigadier
In uniform carrying a tray
Laden with some meringues glacé,
Would saunter forth to feed his birds
Answering their cries with soothing words.
In emulation of their host
His guests regaled the swans with toast
And caviar and tamed the deer
With dry champagne or Munich beer,
But when they asked the cows to lunch,
The thing was caricatured in Punch.

––––––––––

Ah, cruel world of ours! Today,
Lord Water-Cress is put away
And spends his summers, plunged in gloom,
Deserted, in a padded room.
Some friends are there; some others dead.

One shot himself, another fled
To South America with funds,
They say, acquired from German bunds.
The various uncles, sons and aunts
Are all back in their usual haunts,
Including one obstreperous niece
Who is a trial to the police.
The famous Inverness estate,
Complete with sheep and family plate,
Has been bought by a nouveau-riche
Who seldom shaves and smokes hashish,
And who is never, never dined
By anyone at all refined.

In grim conclusion, I must add –
And this is really very sad –
No guests today roam o'er the lawns
With silver spoons to feed the swans,
A fact which no doubt would distress
Lord Abercromby Water-Cress.

THE TROLL

"Pray, have you ever seen a troll?"
Thus at his pupils gibed a droll
Professor, laughing up his sleeve
At the strange things which men believe.

The pupils in dead silence froze
'Till from his seat a youth arose
And said, as if to bare his soul:
"Yes, Doctor, I have seen a troll."

"A troll!" The great professor sneered.
"And did he have a long red beard?
And drink out of an earthen bowl?"
The youth replied: "I saw a troll."

Even a joke goes far enough.
The great professor gave a cough
And said: "Some fiend your wisdom stole.
No one has ever seen a troll."

But, standing up before the class,
The pupil sighed: "Doctor, alas!
He lives, as lives the lowly mole,
Beneath the ground – the dreadful troll!"

Enraged, the great professor cried:
"My friend, the elves and gnomes have died;
The leprechauns hide in a hold."
Then to the class: "THERE IS NO TROLL!"

Swift through the air an arrow sped.
It struck the great professor dead.
But 'ere he reached his distant goal,
He gasped: "The troll! Oh, God – the troll!"

THE YEAR THE BUGS REVOLTED

It's a tradition in New Hampshire that after July four
The bugs and insects disappear and trouble one no more.
But late in May of '69 the insects met, and all
Decided it were better far to hang around 'till Fall.

A million bugs defied with pride New Hampshire's old taboo.
Their motto was: "We'll bite and buzz the whole summer through."
In vain the moderates urged restraint; they could not still the shout,
While angry boos and wild abuse their feeble pleas drowned out.

Boomed Bug Eye, boss of little bugs: "Why should we go away?"
Blared Blue wing, chief of gnats and ticks: "My vote is let us stay!"
Droned Deer Fly, king of things that sting: "Yes, stay and have some fun."
He swooped, bit a tourist who lay snoozing in the sun.

The tourist yelled: "Jehosaphat! I thought you bugs were gone!"
"Oh, no, my friend!" King Deer Fly zinged. "This year we're staying on."
From morn to night the word went: "BITE!" to every tiny pest;
So, on and on, from dusk to dawn the bitten got no rest.

They swatted at the things that swooped; they smeared themselves with grease.
In vain! The hordes with spears and swords gave no one any peace.
Tradition in New Hampshire had received a fatal jolt
In July nineteen sixty-nine, year of the bugs' revolt!

TIME-TABLE

Why is it that when love is sweet
Beneath your peach-green percale sheet,
Here in your penthouse snug and high,
I must get up and say goodbye?

Why, as I hear the muted flow
Of New York traffic far below –
Why, o my sweetheart, must I dress
And leave you in your loveliness?

Let's skip it! – I know the reason why.
Because you are you and I am I,
And your husband's coming at half-past eight...
Hello! – Hey, they tell me his plane is late!

TO A NAGGING WOMAN

You may trail me to my labyrinthine lair;
You may dun me in my den if you dare;
You may grab me at my club
Or trap me in my tub
Or about to rub pomade on my hair.

You may follow me down tortured, twisted paths;
You may seize me while I try on ties at Fath's;
You may (though this is shady!)
Interrupt me with a lady
At a rendezvous in Carcalla's Baths.

You may ask for me from Toots Shor or from Mac;
You may seek me in the slums of Hackensack;
You may search for me in Rome
Or in Paris or at home,
But, Sweetie, I am never coming back!

USNR Versus USN

A senior officer, superb with gold,
His virtues rare and puissant rank extolled,
Blowing cigar smoke in the patient face
Of a Lieutenant with two stripes of lace.
"The time has come," he cried, "to sound the gong
And show you damn reserves where you belong!"

Peace came, and with the ending of the strife,
Some officers returned to private life,
Including the Lieutenant, who once more
Became the gentleman he was before;
While "gentleman" by Act of Congress made
Again were kicked outside the palisade.

Vanished Dream

What is left to remember?
The slither of sea over rocks –
The rattle of wind in December –
The ticking of distant clocks –

The creak of an oar-lock moving –
The whisper of leaves that fall –
The thud of a far door closing –
And – after that – nothing at all!

AMONG FAMILY

A Carter Admirer
On being presented by the Doctor with a Dietary Menu.

O take my hoarded caviar, Beluga's precious grain,
My pâté- from the Strasbourg goose; my lobster fresh from Maine....
Yes, even filch my pheasant pie (I still preserve a little)
Take what you wish — but please, O please! — just leave my peanut brittle!

My Veuve Clicquot, my ris de Veau, my envied Roquefort cheese.....
I can survive — Nay, better, Thrive! — without such things as these.
They only make one grossly fat and needed closets clutter.....
But please — I beg you on my knees — don't take my peanut butter!

That marmalade Escoffier made which has its special shelf
(I sometimes wonder he didn't eat it up himself!)
Well, seize it all !.... But spare one small, small morsel for my lunch ....
For how on earth can one exist without his peanut crunch?

A Carter Admirer
on Being Presented by the
Doctor With a Dietary Menu

O take my hoarded caviar, Beluga's precious grain,

My pâté from the Strasbourg goose; my lobster fresh from Maine...

Yes, even filch my pheasant pie (I still preserve a little)

Take what you wish – but please, <u>o please</u>! – just leave my peanut brittle!

My Veuve Clicquot, my ris de veau, my envied Roquefort cheese...

I can survive – nay, better, thrive! – without such things as these.

They only make one grossly fat and needed closets clutter...

But please – I beg you on my knees – don't take my peanut butter!

That marmalade Escoffier made which has its special shelf

(I sometimes wonder he didn't eat it himself!)

Well, seize it all!... But spare one small, small morsel for my lunch...

For how on earth can one exist without his peanut crunch?

Nelson

Often I've paused in jammed Trafalgar Square
Amid the traffic, to look up and stare
At the small figure perched so very high
He seems to have his niche carved in the sky.
Let qualified historians, I thought,
Tell how that figure lived and loved and fought,
How shall a stranger amplify their story?
How can one add or take from Nelson's glory?

So now I simply sign this little book
Affectionately to Dan, who well may look
For better praise than this in better rhyme —
(My one excuse is that I'm pressed for time)—
The only words I quote today are those
Which Nelson wrote. Not violent or verbose,
Its message holds a kind of quiet beauty:
"England expects every man to do his duty."

                        — Grandaddy

                        Christmas, 1974

Admiral Nelson

Often I've paused in jammed Trafalgar Square
Amid the traffic, to look up and stare
At the small figure perched so very high
He seems to have his niche carved in the sky.
Let qualified historians, I thought,
Tell how that figure lived and loved and fought.
How shall a stranger amplify their story?
How can one add or take from Nelson's glory?

So now I simply sign this little book
Affectionately To Dan, who well may look
For better praise than this in better rhyme—
(My one excuse is that I'm pressed for time)—
The only words I quote today are those
Which Nelson wrote. Not violent or verbose,
His message holds a kind of quiet beauty:
"England expects every man to do his duty."

Grandaddy
Christmas, 1974

All hail, the Derby! Hail, historic race!
With bright flags flying, every colt in place;
Jockeys in crimson silks, in blue, in gold,
In green, in purple — colors manifold
That dazzle and enchant the eager eye;
Trainers and breeders pushing, jostling by;
Smells of the paddock, horseflesh, sweating grooms;
Rich, hearty owners, food in stuffy rooms;
Smells of mint juleps, beaten biscuits, lamb,
Roast turkey, salad, Estill county ham,
Cigar smoke, Chanel number twenty-two.....
Above all other smells (there's quite a few!)
One senses an aroma that brings back
the vanished grandeur of a famous track.

Vague whiffs of glory linger in the air —
Champions that were, but are no longer, there.
Like "Gallant Fox" and long-limbed "Cavalcade"
And Darby Dan's "Proud Clarion" and the shade
Of "Man o' War" whom none has equalled yet,
Nor have we topped the verve of "Calumet",
Nor "Secretariat"'s dash nor that horse with flair —
"Citation", the first equine millionaire —
Names flash like meteors — flaming in their day —
"Count Fleet", "Aristides" and "Whirlaway",
that Indian colt "Black Gold", with Rosa Hoots,
Its Osage owner, sporting English boots;
And don't forget "Dark Star" that Guggenheim
Raced against "Native Dancer" in its prime,
And won the classic, justifying trust
As Vanderbilt (by proxy) bit the dust.
What about "Chateaugay" which reared and shied
When a rose-blanket thorn pierced its sleek hide?
Speaking of roses, who can now recall
"Old Rosebud" trotting grandly to his stall,
Smothered in flowers, while ecstatic cheers
Rang in his breeder's (John E. Madden's) ears?

Today one reads of drugs and cheats and bribes.
The "Courier-Journal" belches diatribes
Against the Derby, while reporters babble
About its great "patricians" and its "rabble".
They tout the Davis Cup, The Super Bowl;
They swallow skiing yarns and nonsense whole;
They've never heard of (or, so it appears)
The noted jockeys of the Derby years —

The Kentucky Derby
The First 100 Years

2.

Sande, Arcaro, Shoemaker or Hartack —
Renowned throughout the world on any racetrack;
They blast the Derby's sordid "avarice",
Ignoring Cobb's remark to Grantland Rice.
Quipped Irvin Cobb, the old Paducah puffin:
"If you ain't seen that race, you ain't seen nuffin"!

~

George Abell
Christmas, 1974

THE KENTUCKY DERBY

All hail, the Derby! Hail, historic race!
With bright flags flying, every colt in place;
Jockeys in crimson silks, in blue, in gold,
In green, in purple – colors manifold
That dazzle and enchant the eager eye;
Trainers and breeders pushing, jostling by;
Smells of the paddock, horseflesh, sweating grooms;
Rich, hearty owners, food in stuffy rooms;
Smells of mint juleps, beaten biscuits, lamb,
Roast turkey, salad, Estill county ham,
Cigar smoke, Chanel number twenty-two.....
Above all other smells (there's quite a few!)
One senses an aroma that brings back
The vanished grandeur of a famous track.

Vague whiffs of glory linger in the air—
Champions that were, but are no longer, there.
Like "Gallant Fox" and long-limbed "Cavalcade"
And Darby Dan's "Proud Clarion" and the shade
Of "Man O' War" whom none has equaled yet,
Nor have we topped the verve of "Calumet,"
Nor "Secretariat"'s dash nor that horse with flair—
"Citation," the first equine millionaire—
Names flash like meteors – flaming in their day—
"Count Fleet", "Aristides" and "Whirlaway",
That Indian colt "Black Gold", with Rosa Hoots,
Its Osage owner, sporting English boots;
And don't forget "Dark Star" that Guggenheim
Raced against "Native Dancer" in its prime,
And won the classic, justifying trust
As Vanderbilt (by proxy) bit the dust.
What about "Chateaugay" which reared and shied
When a rose-blanket thorn pierced its sleek hide?
Speaking of roses, who can now recall
"Old Rosebud" trotting grandly to his stall,
Smothered in flowers, while ecstatic cheers
Rang in his breeder's (John E. Madden's) ears?

Today one reads of drugs and cheats and bribes.
The "Courier-Journal" belches diatribes
Against the Derby, while reporters babble
About its great "patricians" and its "rabble".
They tout the Davis Cup, the Super Bowl;
They swallow skiing yarns and nonsense whole;
They've never heard of (or, so it appears)
The noted jockeys of the Derby years—

2.

Sande, Arcayo, Shoemaker or Hartack—
Renowned throughout the world on any racetrack;
They blast the Derby's sordid "avarice,"
Ignoring Cobb's remark to Grantland Rice.
Quipped Irvin Cobb, the old Paducah puffin:
"If you ain't seen that race, you ain't seen nuffin'"!

~

George Abell
Christmas, 1974

Editor's Note: George Abell was obviously referring to
Eddie Arcaro. Editor chose not to correct his spelling.

Happy Wedding Anniversary

"Sam, Come inside ... and wipe off your feet!
"This T-Bone steak's about ready to eat .....
"Come in! the evening air is cold and wet,
"Our fire is lighted; the table is set
"With our finest china — the jade-green Ming ....
"Come in! Close the door, dear!" said Betty King

Sam closed the door with a puzzled grin.
"What's all this talk of 'Come in, come in'?
"Why do the two dogs stand at salute?
"Why is 'Lucky' dressed in a soldier suit?
"Have you played the horses and picked a winner?
"Or is Grandma Moses coming to dinner?

"Sam dear, you don't mean you can't remember
"What happened long ago in December?
"No, it wasn't the day you met the Queen,
"Nor when you smashed Mother's soup tureen!
"No, it wasn't that time you threw a drink
"Over that cop at the skating rink .....

"You can't remember?...What's that.....No, no!
"It happened just Twenty-eight years ago....
"NO — it wasn't the day they turned you loose
"When you shot a cow instead of a moose!...
"Ah!... At last you remembered!!!...you talked so
"I was just going to call you a chauvinist pig!!"

George Bidell

1975

Happy Writing Anniversary

"Sam come inside... and wipe off your feet!
"This T-Bone steak's about ready to eat...
"Come in! The evening air's cold and wet.
"Our fire is lighted; the table is set
"With our finest china – the jade-green Ming...
"Come in! Close the door, dear!" said Betty King.

Sam closed the door with a puzzled grin,
"What's all this talk of 'come in, come in'?
"Why do the two dogs stand and salute?
"Why is Lucky dressed in a soldier suit?
"Have you played the horses and picked a winner?
"Or is Grandma Moses coming to dinner?

"Sam dear, you don't mean you can't remember
"What happened long ago in December?
"No, it wasn't the day you met the Queen,
"Nor when you smashed Mother's soup tureen!
"No, it wasn't that time you threw a drink
"Over that cop at the skating rink...

"You can't remember?... What's that... <u>No</u>, <u>no</u>!
"It happened just twenty-eight years ago...
"<u>NO</u> – it wasn't the day they turned you loose
"When you shot a cow instead of a moose!
"Ah!... At last you remembered!!!... You talked so big
"I was just going to call you a chauvinist pig!"

George Abell
1973

L.A.

Ruffles

I never knew him in his prime,
So through my dreams he shuffles —
A dear old, still bold pet. His name,
Incongruously, was "Ruffles"!

I hear again his vibrant bark,
His growls, his snorts and snuffles.
I visualize him somewhat lame —
A slightly battered "Ruffles".

But, young or old or hale or lame,
No dream his image muffles.
Time cannot ever dim nor mar
My memory of "Ruffles".

George Abell.
Christmas, 1975

RUFFLES

I never knew him in his prime,
So through my dreams he shuffles –
A dear old, still bold pet. His name,
Incongruously, was "Ruffles!"

I hear again his vibrant bark,
His growls, his snorts and snuffles.
I visualize him somewhat lame –
A slightly battered "Ruffles."

But, young or old or hale or lame,
No dream his image muffles.
Time cannot ever dim nor mar
My memory of "Ruffles."

George Abell
Christmas, 1975

The Arrival of Mr. Abell

It was 6:45. Through the hospital
    hall the twilight was tenderly gleaming.
One heard not a sound, save the orderly's round and a few
    patients quietly screaming.
Some nurses, half-drugged by the wonderful calm, piled bandages up
    on a table.
Then a sudden great yell broke the mystical spell:
"My name, sir, is **Dan Tyler Abell**."

From whence came that cry? Is it here?
    Was it there?
Oh, what were the words it was booming?
Five Doctors ran out of a ward as that shout
    again set the echoes a-zooming.

"My name is not Jack, is not Harry or Dick! It's surely not Martha or Mabel!
"Just look at that clock! Hey, leggo of me, Doc! My name, sir,
"Is **Dan Tyler Abell!**"

An alarm shrieked a warning, policemen arrived ... They
    demanded: "Well, where is the body?"
The shocked superintendent (from fear independent)
    stood nervously gulping a toddy.
Around him surged interns and nurses and nuts —
    a regular Tower of Babel.
Yet still, through that crowd rang that voice harsh and loud —
"My name, sir, is **Dan Tyler Abell!**"

A scientist wise in a place far away from that scene of terrific endeavour
Worked late in the night and (although slightly tight) studied (a
    thing which he did hardly ever).
At last he looked up from the paper he wrote and sighed, "I
    must send them a cable,
"My augur is here; he's the man of the year, and the
    name ... Well, it's Dan Tyler Abell!"

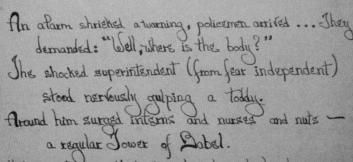

THE ARRIVAL OF MR. ABELL

It was 6:45. Through the hospital hall the twilight was tenderly gleaming.

One heard not a sound, save the orderly's round and a few

patients quietly screaming.

Some nurses, half-drugged by the wonderful calm, piled bandages

up on a table.

Then a sudden great yell broke the mystical spell:

"My name, sir, is **Dan Tyler Abell**."

From whence came that cry? Is it here? Was it there? Oh, what were

the words it was booming?

Five doctors ran out of a ward as that shout again set the echoes a-zooming.

"My name is not Jack, is not Harry or Dick! It's surely not Martha or Mabel!

"Just look at that clock! Hey, leggo of me, Doc!

"My name, sir, is **Dan Tyler Abell!**"

An alarm shrieked a warning, policemen arrived...They demanded:

"Well where is the body?"

The shocked superintendent (from fear independent) stood

nervously gulping a toddy.

Around him surged interns and nurses and nuts—a regular Tower of Babel.

Yet still, through that crowd rang that voice harsh and loud—

"My name, sir, is **Dan Tyler Abell!**"

A scientist wise in a place far away from that scene of terrific endeavor

Worked late in the night and (although slightly tight) studied (a thing

which he did hardly ever).

At last he looked up from the paper he wrote and sighed,

"I must send them a cable,

"My augur is here; he's the man of the year,

And the name...Well, it's **Dan Tyler Abell**."

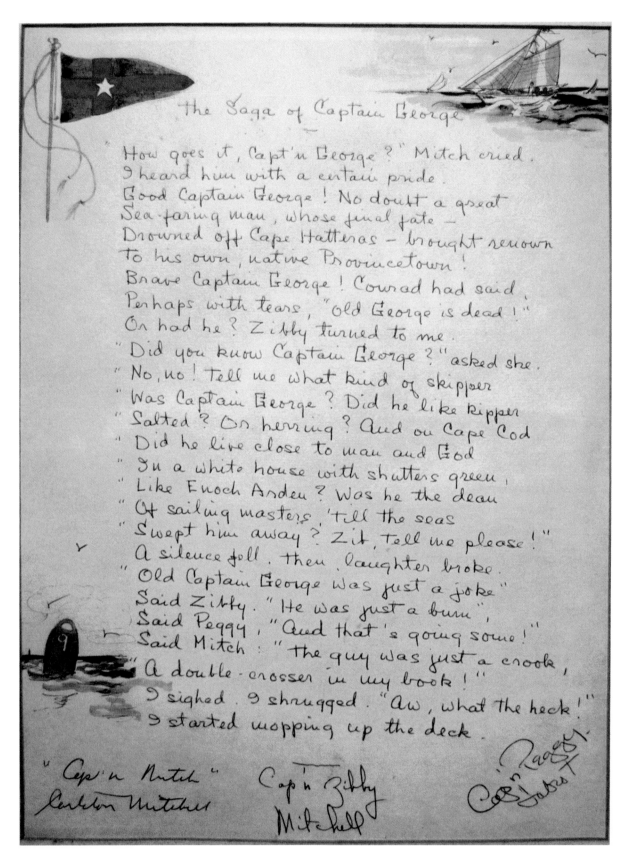

the Saga of Captain George

"How goes it, Capt'n George?" Mitch cried.
I heard him with a certain pride.
Good Captain George! No doubt a great
Sea-faring man, whose final fate –
Drowned off Cape Hatteras – brought renown
To his own, native Provincetown!
Brave Captain George! Conrad had said,
Perhaps with tears, "Old George is dead!"
Or had he? Zibby turned to me.
"Did you know Captain George?" asked she.
"No, no! Tell me what kind of skipper
"Was Captain George? Did he like kipper
"Salted? Or herring? And on Cape Cod
"Did he live close to man and God
"In a white house with shutters green,
"Like Enoch Arden? Was he the dean
"Of sailing masters, 'till the seas
"Swept him away? Z it, Tell me please!"
A silence fell. then laughter broke.
"Old Captain George was just a joke"
Said Zibby. "He was just a bum",
Said Peggy, "And that's going some!"
Said Mitch: "The guy was just a crook,
"A double-crosser in my book!"
I sighed. I shrugged. "Aw, what the heck!"
I started mopping up the deck.

"Cap'n Mitch"
Carleton Mitchell

Cap'n Zibby
Mitchell

Peggy
Cap'n Jabes

Editor's Note: The people who signed this poem are Carleton Mitchell, his wife Libby, and Peggy Labrodt. Carleton Mitchell was the only person to ever win the renowned Newport-Bermuda Race three years in a row (in a thirty-nine-foot yawl named Finisterre). Peggy Labrodt, a friend of George Abell, was the widow of Ed Labrodt – another famous sailor.

THE SAGA OF CAPTAIN GEORGE

"How goes it, Capt'n George?" Mitch cried.
I heard him with a certain pride.
Good Captain George! No doubt a great
Sea-faring man, whose final fate—
Drowned off Cape Hatteras—brought renown
To his own, native Provincetown!
Brave Captain George! Conrad had said,
Perhaps with tears, "Old George is dead!"
Or had he? Zibby turned to me.
"Did you know Captain George?" asked she.
"No, no! Tell me what kind of skipper
'Was Captain George? Did he like kipper
"Salted? Or herring? And on Cape Cod
"Did he live close to man and God
"In a white house with shutters green,
"Like Enoch Ardeu? Was he the dean
"Of sailing masters, 'till the seas
"Swept him away? Zib, tell me please!"
A silence fell. Then laughter broke.
"Old Captain George was just a joke"
Said Zibby. "He was just a bum"
Said Peggy, "And that's going some!"
Said Mitch: "The guy was just a crook,
"A double-crosser in my book!"
I sighed. I shrugged. "Aw, what the heck!"
I started mopping up the deck.

Bess - with love from George.

Mr. George Abell

with l...
Bess -

!

G.A.

George Abell

Mr. George Abell

To a Raccoon.

When the frost of Winter shines
On the henhouse and the pines,
The sly raccoon adjusts his mask
And goes about his nightly task,
Which is, precisely, to vamoose
With anything that's lying loose.....
A crust of bread, a piece of string,
A rake, an old tire — anything.
No snow's too deep, no barn too draughty
To stop this rambler cool and crafty.
He gets the loot he's looking for
While sleepy victims calmly snore
Then wake to find that while they've slept
The cunning burglar's taken all except
The **roof** and left no single trace
Of worrying paw or smiling face!

Well, let him go! His petty crimes
Are symptomatic of our times
And far more fair than those we meet
Out on the highway or the street
He steals for food and Winter shelter,
Scattering the refuse helter-skelter,
Leaving the garden, I confess,
In an appalling, dreadful mess.
So what?... Most visitors, you'll find,
Do just the same. They'll drink you blind,
Then rush off, leaving in their wake
Crushed cigarettes on slabs of cake,
Half-empty glasses, plus a lot
Of trash and trivia they forgot.

Come when you like, cute little falla!
You will not leave a wet umbrella
Or garbage clogging up the sink —
And, best of all, you never drink!

G.A.

TO A RACCOON

When the frost of Winter shines
On the henhouse and the pines,
The sly raccoon adjusts his mask
And goes about his nightly task,
Which is, precisely, to vamoose
With anything that's lying loose.....
A crust of bread, a piece of string,
A rake; an old tire—anything.
No snow's too deep, no barn too draughty
To stop this rambler cool and crafty.
He gets the loot he's looking for
While sleeping victims calmly snore
Then wake to find that while they've slept
The cunning burglar's taken all except
The roof and left no single trace
Of worrying paw or smiling face!

Well, let him go! His petty crimes
Are symptomatic of our times
And far more fair than those we meet
Out on the highway or the street
He steals for food and Winter shelter,
Scattering the refuse helter-skelter,
Leaving the garden, I confess,
In an appalling, dreadful mess.
So what?...Most visitors, you'll find,
Do just the same. They'll drink you blind,
Then rush off, leaving in their wake
Crushed cigarettes on slabs of cake,
Half-empty glasses, plus a lot
Of trash and trivia they forgot.

Come when you like, cute little fella!
You will not leave a wet umbrella
Or garbage clogging up the sink—
And, best of all, you never drink!

Unnamed Poem by Charles S. Abell (1876-1953)

Farewell you bums, and loafers too,

I am forever done with you.

Your hot air gags and jokes profane

Have nearly driven me insane.

But now at last my time has come.

I leave my work and start to bum.

Your hoodlum voices and your yell

Are over now – farewell farewell.

Charles S. Abell was George Abell's father who
penned this verse on the occasion of his resignation
as managing editor of the Sun Papers of Baltimore. -- Ed.

EARLY PUBLISHED VERSE

"The trouble with the present arrangement extends even to the various kinds of bears. The polar bears are under the Department of Commerce, the grizzly bears are under the Department of the Interior, and the brown bears are under the Department of Agriculture."

–Secretary of Commerce Herbert Hoover in an
address before the National Press Club.

Is It Bearable?

The polar, brown or grizzly bear is neatly classified,
And ranked by Governmental clerks according to his hide.

Thus one becomes a Hooverite; another goes to Fall,
While "Bears what hae wi' Wallace bled" is bruin's dinner call.

But where stands Ursus Cinnamon, the wildest in the Zoo?
Pray, have we no department which can regulate him, too?

Would not the diplomatic corps, or 'folio of State,
Be just the sort of guardians for a wily reprobate?

The Treasury Department might give him a wider range,
And let him chase the bulls about the New York Stock Exchange!

Or possibly our Congress could provide a safe retreat,
With harbor loans and Sunday laws and Senators to eat!

The Teddy Bear has passed away—the Russian bear's a jest—
O, for the honor of the land, let us preserve the rest!

Paste This in Your Hat for Next New Year's Eve

Huroo! Huree! Bring butter, slave, and vintage from the oaken jug.
The rose leaf springs from Omar's grave, and Cleopatra sheds her rug.

Before yon frosty moon has set behind the mansion of the mayor,
A merry toot of silver horns shall rouse the dormouse from its lair.

Let cymbals clang and cellos throb the sleepy night to loud applause!
Upon the cloth, this crimson blob, proclaims our scorn of Volstead's laws.

Et Tu, Bore?

One hears the average man complain
About the tariff and the rain,
But you'll agree when I deplore
Above all other ills—the bore.

Is it not sad for etiquette
To so enmesh us in its net
That we must bear with debutantes,
And Bolsheviks and maiden aunts?

Why is it we're allowed to rope
The law-abiding antelope,
While judges rule the bore is not
The sort of creature to be shot?

Yet, even though it seems a shame
To know that bores are not free game,
The author's rather lucky, for
Some one might call this verse a bore.

FASHION

The king rides slowly down the Strand,
A black kid glove on either hand—
So black kid gloves advance to twice
Their normal proletarian price!

The king adopts a gray felt hat,
Or puts a pearl in his cravat,
And lo—One cannot choose but pay
Outrageous sums for pearly gray.

Thus fashion baits a world of fops,
With little royal lollypops,
And we'd wear whiskers to the grave
If once the king forgot to shave.

THE CAT'S ANKLE

He saw an ankle, slim and neat,
Picking its way across the street;
But instead of "Hello," he called out, "Scat!"
And tossed a stone at the wandering cat.

OH, WAITER!

"A cantaloupe pudding," the young man cried,
But the waiter was kissing the maid.
He haughtily turned to the guest and replied:
"The cantaloupe pudding is dead."

"It died, sir, at midnight. I stood by the corpse,
And wept as they carried it out,
My soul for the moment was filled with remorse,
And horrible feelings of doubt."

"But why?" asked the other, "pray what did you care?"
The waiter grew pale as a ghost.
He gave the inquirer a murderous glare,
With eyes that resembled milk toast.

"I alone–," he began, but broke off at the word,
As he gargled and gurgled for breath.
It seems the head waiter had entered unheard
And was choking the poor chap to death.

CHESS

Professor Binks and Mr. Jinks
Were playing chess,
While on their way to Lord-knows-where
On the 3:45 Express.

The landscape glided swiftly by.
"Check," said Professor Binks.
The engineer saw five cows on the track.
"Your move," said Mr. Jinks.

The engineer jumped for his life;
Binks moved the bishop's pawn.
With a roar the train plunged down the bank,
Rolling on and on.

Professor Binks and Mr. Jinks
Lay silently side by side;
Finally Jinks opened his eyes and said:
"Checkmate," and then he died.

THE QUEST OF SCHUCH

Concerning Adolph Schuch, Commissioner of Street Cleaning.

I plodded through the cloud of dust
That rose in quaint, exotic swirls,
Enveloped limousine and truck,
And choked the cops and pretty girls.

But as I stumbled through the dirt,
With many a knock or angry push,
A stranger seized me by the shirt,
And cried: "I seek for one called Schuch!"

"My friend," said I, "your search is in vain,
Why waste your life on such a trail?"
He sadly shook his head and moaned:
"King Arthur sought the Holy Grail.

"Young Jason sought the Golden Fleece,
And Menelaus sought his queen,
Why should not I seek Mr. Schuch,
To make your dirty city clean?"

"But pray consider, sir," said I,
"The handsome street o'er which we roam";
"Alas," the stranger made reply,
"I left my spectacles at home."

TO A PROFITEER

Your father was a butcher, I am told;
Your mother took in washing by the week;
Yet your shaving mug is made of solid gold
And you have a diamond collar on your peke.

The livery all your negro servants bear
Is of a more aristocratic hue
Than that your foolish uncle had to wear
When he was sent to jail in '92.

I frankly vow I do not understand
The coat-of-arms that glistens on your gate.
As I remember it, your family brand
Was generally observed upon a plate.

Still, after all, you have your cellar keys,
Your horses and your houses and your health;
You can afford to let the F. F. V.'s
Sneer at your vulgar, three-times envied wealth.

THE MOLOSSIAN PUPPY

When drowsy dreams my senses clog
I draw a chair before the fire
And gaze at my Molossian dog—
(An animal you would admire).

It stands upon the mantelpiece,
Between a chip of Windsor plate
And sketches of my uncle's niece
As she appeared in '88.

How soothing are its massive jaws,
That gleam serenely in the light;
But scarcely could be used because
A china tooth will seldom bite.

Some day (if you like tea or gin,
Or maybe only gingerale),
I hope, perhaps, you'll venture in;
Just watch my puppy wag its tail!

AN APPEAL

LOST—One hedgehog, mouse-colored. Very fond of beetles.
(The most pathetic of many sad cases brought to the attention
of the city's charitable institutions.)

"My hedgehog," is the old man's plea—
"Oh, bring my hedgehog back to me!"

For many days his tears like rain
Have fallen on the basement floor,
Where once his valiant hog has slain
Resplendent beetles by the score.

Since hedgehogs, as you doubtless know,
Delight in crunching beetles black,
And it has made the old man glow
To watch his creature on their track.

But now, alas, in angry droves
Around his bench the beetles swarm.
Their breath is hot as fiery stoves,
The poor old man feels very warm.

Mayhap his hedgehog, thinly gauzed,
Is wandering through a city street—
It may have died from surfeit caused
By all the bugs it used to eat.

Will you not heed an old man's whim
And bring his hedgehog back to him?

GOTT MIT HUNS!

Come weep with me, ye crocodiles, that bask upon the River Rhine.
"Der Vaterland! Der Vaterland!" I hear your deprecating whine.
Alas! must Germans pay their debts, instead of buying Swedish stocks,
And shall the barons on the Ruhr no longer hold the treasure box?

"Inhuman—cruel," cries out the press. "Outrageous," shrieks the moron mob.
Quite right! When burglars steal our plate, let us forgive the ones who rob.
Let us forget the ruined homes, the ravaged lands, the dismal war.
Why worry over mere details, such as ten million marks or more?

Those rows of crosses at Verdun have not the sentiment of old,
And Belgium's rape you must admit is scarcely worth a ton of gold.
So, crocodiles, come weep with me! My falling teardrops, I protest,
Have nearly washed the German dyes out of my new imported vest!

SHE BLOWS!

The captain strolled along the deck
And eyed the placid ocean.
"A whale! A whale!" the lady cried,
Good heavens, what a commotion!

"Quick, madam! Show me where it blows.
Yo, ho! Avast! Ahoy"
He bellowed orders to the crew
And cursed the cabin boy.

They took the grappling irons out,
And dipped them in the water.
The first lieutenant seized the mast
And tied it to his daughter.

"But, madam, madam! Where's the whale?"
"Why, captain, can't you find it?
It's lying almost at your feet,
Do take a rope and bind it."

Across the bridge a sailor stepped,
And (frightful tortures braving)
He kicked the flying-fish o'erboard,
And then resumed his shaving.

ODE TO A SEALSKIN COAT

O floppy, sloppy seal, from the regions of the North,
You brave the bergs of Bergen and the choppy Arctic seas,
And you're penned in zoos and gardens by a lot of stupid wardens,
And your fur is used to cover up a debby's silken knees!

O squeaky, sleeky seal, you no longer romp and bark
Where the frozen, shiny fishes lure the slashing polar bear.
You are now a fur of fashion and your most absorbing passion
Is to trail across a ballroom or to grace an opera chair.

O happy, wrappy seal, though you'll never flip again,
And Aurora Borealis gleams no longer for your eyes,
You would rather screen a lady, we are sure, than lead a shady
And rather wild existence under cold Alaskan skies.

THE WAITER AND THE ALLIGATOR

'Neath the sultry sun of noon,
In a Florida lagoon,
    Basks the alligator;
'Neath the palms and potted plants,
Of our Southern restaurants,
    Lurks the waiter.

With his elongated teeth,
He will eat you like roast beef,
    Will the alligator;
With his sickly little grin,
He will scoop your money in,
    Will the waiter.

If I had to choose between
The crocodile and Paris green,
    And the waiter,
I'd take the poison "off the bat"
And after that,
    The alligator.

DECLINING AN INVITATION TO A PICNIC

Rave not to me of potted roast
    Beneath the oak tree's branches,
Where insects melt in buttered toast
    And girls' audacious glances.

I'd rather kiss some charming lass
    Who's never seen a spider,
Than lunch with one who doubtless has
    A score or so inside her.

SKI!

(In spite of the popularity of the Chauve Souris, this was reluctantly passed by the censor.)

'Twas Ivanoff, the Samovar, that played a verst on his ukraine:
"Most lovely Vodka, be my bride and heed my mujik's pleading strain;
The antlered Omsk graze sadly, dear, outside my Pogrom's massive gate,
While Tomsk, my moscow, barks in vain to greet the Vodka I await.

"O, won't you wear your kremlin dress, and trotsky to the priest with me?
Must I siberia all day, while you seem droshky to my plea?
Arcangel—listen to my prayer and tell me ikon understand;
Okhotsk, with love, I kneel today, and bolshevikly ask your hand."

But Vodka shook her pretty curls and whispered this to Ivanoff:
"O, Ruble youth, you waste your time. Farewell! For I must romanoff!"
She caroled blithely down the road, and Ivanoff was in despair
To see a nevsky prospect place a gold ivostchik in her hair!

LATER PUBLISHED VERSE

THE DINOSAUR THAT DREAMED OF SPROUTING WINGS

"A party from the American Museum of Natural History traveled last week by jeep and trailer into the San Juan basin of northern New Mexico. In its beds of brown rock they hope to find fossils of the phytosaur, thought to be the remote ancestor of all the dinosaurs and remarkably like the unrelated modern crocodile."—*Newsweek*

IN PREHISTORIC times, beside
An ocean grey and rough and wide,
There roamed a baby dinosaur
Who found his life a wretched bore.
His parents had been eaten by
A brontosaurus on the sly,
Which left him only Uncle Bill,
Unsympathetic, old and ill,
Plus two small cousins, Joe and Pete,
Who measured scarcely 50 feet,
And weren't the kind of creatures that
He could invite for a chat.

AND so along the ocean shore
This lonely baby dinosaur
Strolled for about 500 years,
Moping and yawning, bathed in tears.
Each year or so he ate a meal
Of monster shark and giant seal,
While storms that raged upon the deep
Lulled him into a month of sleep.
But usually his tear-dimmed eye
Followed the mammoth butterfly
That fluttered past in heavy droves
Above the ocean's rocky coves.
"Ah, me," the dinosaur would muse,
"If only I had wings, I'd choose
Lightly to vault into the blue
Far, far away into some new

And better world, if such there be!"
Then, drinking up a lake for tea,
He'd sob until his tears of pain
Had filled the lake right up again.

ONCE, as he pondered, thin and low—
He'd lost 1,000 tons or so—
He fell asleep, and in a dream
Saw frightful visions that did seem
Gigantic horrors...tubes of flame...
Huge birds that roared and put to shame
The pterodactyls...bursts of fire...
Weird beasts that fought in swamps and mire...
Lightnings that hurled out of the blue
And clove a shrieking world in two...
The dinosaur in fear awoke,
Seized with his toes a mighty oak
And, bellowing in agony,
Tossed it far out into the sea,
Moaning at thought of what he'd seen.
"Lucky," he cried, "that I have been
Spared from such nightmares! Were they real
I should indeed have cause to squeal!"

FROM that time on his mood became
Angelic, Amiable and tame,
He romped with cousins Joe and Pete,
(Who measured now 100 feet)
And even pleased his Uncle Bill
By bringing him a jumbo pill
Designed to banish heart distress
In half a century or less.
So gay was he that in his youth
He frolicked with the Sabre Tooth—
That loathsome tiger who was banned
By every fossil in the land,
And was by law forbid to roam

Near any antediluvian home.
He was, in brief, the perfect gent
Of phytosaurian descent.
He called the eohippus friend,
Though jealous saurians did pretend
He cultivated him to get
Accepted by the horsey set.

AT ANY rate, he lived for aeons,
And everybody sang his paeans
When, flourishing a snow-white beard,
Venerable, gentle and revered,
He sank serenely to a grave
Beneath the crooning ocean wave.
So rolled the world and so time past
Till in our century at last
A wise professor found a trace
Of that poor dinosaur whose grace,
Whose kindness and beatitude
Had proved so fine an interlude
In prehistoric days. The prof,
Taking his coat and waistcoat off,
Exclaimed with joy: "A dinosaur!
Well, men, what are we waiting for?"
Loud cheered the crew. They dug and dug.
A bone...a skull...They gave a tug,
And there, exposed to human eyes,
Reposed a form of massive size.

THE wise professor gave a roar:
"One thousand feet," he yelled, "or more!
Observe the fierce, protruding jowl—
The dreadful teeth bared in a scowl!
What jaws! What crushing, grasping feet!
No pleasant animal to meet,
I'll wager, for a cave-man who
Lingered too late in evening dew"

But one lone student, standing by,
Remarked: "Professor, maybe I
Am wrong, and yet it looks as if
Those jaws, by centuries made stiff
Tend to a sort of ghastly smile."
"What!" cried the prof. "This beast so vile,
So dangerous, ravenous for food,
Was NEVER in a pleasant mood."
He added: "In that awful age
There was, of course, no learned sage
To tell us what such monsters thought.
Most probably they dreamed of naught
Except to kill, nor guessed how we
Live in our present century."

OUR STATE DEPARTMENT BOYS

How cheering in these horrid times of knavery and fraud
To realize that Uncle Sam is being served abroad
By a bevy of cherubic gents whom Jimmy Byrnes employs—
Our complaisant, cultivated, lovely State Department Boys!

What matters it if treachery be rampant in the East?
(I really doubt if Chiang Kai-shek wears trousers neatly creased!)
And Hurley's revelations? Tush! Away with all that noise!
Let's place our hopes for safety in our State Department Boys!

They'll soothe our English debtors with a cup of India tea;
They'll daunt those Russian peasants with a dash of sophistry.
O woe to foreign quibbling when Dean Acheson deploys
Our ingratiating, tactful, gallant State Department Boys!

They flit with elegance about the mansions of the great,
Discussing with uplifted brows the problems of the state.
Why, Archibald MacLeish himself cannot approach the poise,
The grace, the charm, the MANNER of our State Department Boys!

It's nice to think of them in Rome and even in Hong Kong—
Where doubtless they are helping us by sipping old Souchong.
I'm certain Indonesia, too, emphatically enjoys
Our polished, suave, but—oh, so cunning– State Department Boys!

Manchuria? They know it not. The atom business?—Nix!
But, gracious, aren't they wizards at internal politics!
They'll lure an aide memoire—(The scamps!)—with cocktails as decoys—
Our artful, devilish, lynx-eyed, tricky State Department Boys!

They're affable and sociable to potentate and pope,
And ALWAYS quite immaculate! (It's Buffy Kirk's own soap!)
So, to hell with Stalin's mujhiks in their greasy corduroys!
Let's string along with Jimmy and our State Department Boys!

ON GETTING UP

(After 3 years of being on daily Navy duty at 8 a.m.)

I admire, in a faint, philosophical way,
Those persons who leap from the covers each day.
Being roused by alarm clocks or bugles or bells
Or sergeants who give the most terrible yells.
I respect—with a touch of disdainful reserve—
Those creatures all brimming with sunshine and verve
Who sing in cold showers; then, light a cigar;
Give a pat to the dog as they jump in the car,
And arrive at the office a picture of glee,
Whistling tunes out of "Pinafore" badly off key—
So blithe, so elated by bacon and eggs,
By waffles, by orange juice drained to the dregs—
So blissful and cordial it does your heart good.
(At least, if it doesn't, it certainly should!)
I tolerate even those dopes who awake
And immediately order a buffalo steak
With hashed brown potatoes all sizzingly fried
And pancakes and lots of whipped cream on the side
And hot buttered rum in an extra big cup...
Well, it's not my idea of the way to get up!
Now, me—I'm a sensible sort of a guy.
I rise when the sun has been long in the sky.
Of course, it's too late for those miserable birds,
So all that I hear are some menial's words
Inquiring how long I'm remaining in bed.
Of course, there's the usual pain in my head;
The throb in my ears and the twitch in my eye,
Plus the usual belief that I'm going to die—
And it better be quick...But the feeling's soon past
And glorious solace engulfs me at last!
With two bromo-seltzers, a grain of quinine
And injections of sulfa the future looks fine;

Then some jasmine bouquet in my steaming hot tub
And some Coty de Chypre in my alcohol rub;
A gargle of pine needles, glycerin and gin;
A deft touch of eau-de-cologne to my chin;
Three cups of black coffee, twelve vitamin pills;
A brandy, a lemon without any frills;
A dash of some drug in a honey-dipped roll—
A raw egg in claret (just swallow it whole!)...
Ah, now!...foie de vivre; The blood in my vein
Is as bubbling and fresh as that glass of champagne
I invariably gulp before sauntering forth
To the West or the South or the East or the North!

TELL ME NOT, TENNYSON

O tell me not, Tennyson, tales of the sea
That breaks with a roar on the rocks!
You never, Lord Alfred, have listened like me
To the roar of Congressional blocs!

And, Shelley, your skylark is frankly absurd
Compared to the eloquence pouring
From the lips that belong to a far different Byrd—
Even though I admit he's not soaring!

You poets who glorify wind in the trees
Have never heard Pepper's discussions!
And why rave of murmuring waters and bees
When here we have murmuring Russians?

Pray what is the sound of a pattering tot
To the pattering, puttering Ickes?
Can Gray's "lowing cattle" compete with a lot
Of lobbyists gulping gin rickeys?

Contrasts

In this great Capital
If you don't nap at all
And if you lap a tall
Whiskey & soda wherever you roam
You'll find hilarity
Plus popularity
And, as a rarity,
You'll dine at home.
If, for variety,
You try sobriety,
So-called society
Such arrant piety will not condone.
You'll find economy
Studying agronomy,
Greek and astronomy,
Dining alone.

Cads!

I do not care for persons who
Behind your back speak ill of you;
But I consider a disgrace
Those who insult you to your face.

THE EASTER RABBIT HABIT

I MUCH DEPLORE this stupid habit
Of worshipping the Easter Rabbit.
We set him up in stores and shops
And model him in lollipops
And paint his face on Easter eggs
And ties and cards and women's legs.
You find him everywhere you walk;
On walls and fences, traced in chalk—
In drugstore windows, stuffed and fat—
On some outrageous Easter hat—
On candy boxes blue and pink—
On posters done in Chinese ink—
In gay, artistic rug designs—
In ads for California wines—
On catsup labels, seals and crests—
On quaint, enameled Easter chests—
Why, even in my verse appears
That Rabbit's sickening smirk—and ears!
What has he others haven't got?
To hell with him! He should be shot!

THE APPIAN WAY

Said Appius Claudius to his son:
"In Rome hard drinking isn't done."
Said Appius Junior: "Still, I think
"That I am 'appius when I—hic!—drink!"

SKI!

'Twas Ivanoff, the Samovar, that played a verst on his ukraine:
"Most lovely Vodka, be my bride and heed my mujik's pleading strain!
The antlered omsk graze sadly, dear, outside my pogrom's massive gate
While Tomsk, my moscow, barks in vain to greet the Vodka I await.

"O won't you wear your kremlin dress and trotsky to the priest with me?
Must I siberia all day while you seem droshky to my plea?
Archangel, hearken to my prayer and answer: 'Ikon understand!'
Okhotsk with love I kneel today and bolshevikly ask your hand."

But Vodka, smiling, shook her curls and thus replied to Ivanoff:
"O ruble youth, you waste your time. Farewell, for I must romanoff!
This cossak, piled with scarlet grapes, must be delivered 'ere they sour
To one who may become—who knows?—a nevsky prospekt in an hour."

DIPLOMATIC DIALOGUE

I thought he had Eurasian looks
So tried him out in Greek,
But found he'd learned his French from books
And that his Czech was weak.

In Lapp and Finn we sought to chin—
Although his Swedish much
Superior to my Russian proved
And better than my Dutch.

Next, Polish adjectives he'd shout;
Then Spanish dialects—
But all this language whisked about
Served only to perplex.

Into my native tongue I broke
(A diplomatic crime!)
And—strike me dumb—I found he spoke
Good English all the time!

APPENDIX

(Dedicated to my friend, Willmott Lewis, Jr., convalescent)

When famous surgeons operate
They never, never hesitate.
An instant's pause may be the breath
Between a patient's life and death.

The wire arrives: "APPENDIX BAD."
Signed: "OSCAR HENDRIX BLOTTINGPAD."
At once the surgeon grabs a knife,
Barks quick instructions to his wife:

"It's Blottingpad...financial bet...
"Amazing man...I'll save him, pet...
"Get me those drugs...It's six o'clock.
"Look up the planes from Little Rock!"

A second wire: "APPENDIX WORSE."
The famous surgeon sends a nurse,
Packs up a grip, wires back "HOLD TIGHT"
And vanishes from human sight.

Then, two days later from Quebec
Or Reno or Tehuantepec
The news is flashed: "APPENDIX BURST.
"DEATH, NOT DOCTOR, GETS HERE FIRST."

LAMENT FOR QUEEN VICTORIA

In Victoria's day – which, alas, is no more—
One ordered the landau at half after four
And, with coach dogs exhibiting delicate grace,
Drove out to some fashionable watering place.
There was plenty of time; there was money to spare.
Barometers pointed to "sunny and fair".
To die was unpleasant; to live was a lark.
The violets were all coming out in the park.
O Lord, what a day! What a leisurely time,
O Lord, when Victoria was in her prime!

I muse on that era of vapors and whims
When women had bustles and corsets and "limbs";
When candles were pink-shaded, whiskers were waxed
And only the third footman's livery was taxed.
If you went on a diet, your average lunch
Consisted of terrapin, truffles and punch,
With maybe a touch of incredible port
Which you'd buy now for $22 a quart.
O Lord, what a day! What a wonderful time,
O Lord, when Victoria was in her prime!

I dream of that actress with plumes in her hat
Who was simply enchanted to sup at your flat;
Of gold-headed canes and poodles and pugs;
Of flashy cigars and impossible rugs;
I vision a waistcoat embroidered in pearls
That I'd nervously twirl as I ogled the girls
Who'd coyly smile with a half-fearful glance
At the shepherding escort of uncles and aunts.
O Lord, what a day! What a fanciful time,
O Lord, when Victoria was in her prime!

LET US EAT CAKE!

"Relief Grain to be loaned to make Bread for Americans"...
"Britons face 7-slices-daily Bread Ration"...

—Newspaper headlines, June 4, 1946

O English Cousins, at whose teas
I've gorged on many a tasty muffin,
Can it be true that overseas
You now have...nuffin?

Need humble 'clarks' and belted earls
Go almost supperless to bed?
Need duchesses and chorus girls
Eat only bread?

I rise, dear Cousins, to proclaim
That famished England still shall live,
While we—quite obviously to blame—
Must give...and give!

London shall have her buttered scones
Although our cities thrive on crust,
And barley loaves build English bones,
Though starve we must!

And if perchance, to our regret,
Our bakers will no longer bake,
Why – Shades of Marie Antoinette! –
Let us eat cake!

ODE TO THE U.S. FOREIGN POLICY
(IF ANY)

Hi, little policy!
Are you a fallacy?
Have you a heart or a core?
Are you alive and real?
Are you a spinning wheel?
Who in the hell are you for?

Are you a butterfly
Flitting through Uruguay?
Are you a fact in Madrid
Or Argentina with
Dear Mr. Messersmith?
Whom are you trying to kid?

Are you for unity
In one community
And for dissension in others?
And yet not comprehend
Stalin and Peron are brothers?

Will you with Connally
Wrestle phenomenally
Over our foreign affairs?
Or with the Groton swells
Will you cheer Sumner Welles
Kicking Spruille Braden downstairs?

Are you for Hull or Byrnes?
Are you a vane that turns?
Are you a myth or a "maybe"?
May I, with self-restraint,
Say: "Is you is or ain't?
Is you whose policy, baby?"

THE LIBERAL COLUMNIST AND THE CONSERVATIVE OCTOPUS

A modern periodical
Of new ideas symbolical,
Decided on an article
Unusual and weird;
So it sent out (by ship and bus)
A man to meet an Octopus
And find out what the creature was,
And if it wore a beard;
And if it waxed hermitical
Or purely parasitical;
To which advanced political
Opinions it adhered.

The Columnist (God pity us!)
A Liberal – and poisonous –
Went out and spied the Octopus
A-basking in the sea.
He fired at it his questionnaire,
To which the monster, debonair,
And blowing bubbles in the air,
Said: "Stranger, look at me!
"Observe my every tentacle,
"Authentical, identical!
"I'd wind them 'round your ventricle
"As easy as could be.

"My traits have such variety
"That frankly my society
"Is not revered with piety
"By people hereabout.
"In fact, sir, you may summon all
"Sea animals phenomenal;
"My qualities abdominal
"Will fast put them to rout.
"My inky black fluidity

"Soon conquers all lucidity,
"I pity his stupidity
"Who too late finds it out."

The Liberal Columnist, agog
At his octopian monologue,
Replied: "You might be in a fog
"To boast that ink you squirt.
"You prate, dear friend, of hideous,
"Invidious, insidious,
"Contrivances amphibious
"Designed to kill and hurt;
"But you can't touch the slimeiness,
"The all-pervading grimeiness,
"The devilish, clever timeliness
"With which I spew my dirt."

The Octopus, now sickly blue,
Gasped: "Brother, I have heard of you.
"Forgive my sudden change of hue,
"But I am not a 'pink'.
"Your theories astronomical,
"Your diatribes most comical,
"Your frolics anatomical,
"In my opinion, stink.
"I've watched your grotesque pantomime,
"And – though a monster maritime –
"If you're a Liberal, then I'm
"Conservative, I think!"

BALLADE OF THE SUPREME COURT

I sing the Justices of old—
Their virtues rare yet manifold!
Mere men who, if the truth be told,
Their prejudices kept!
Yet, valiant despite prejudice,
They made our system what it is.
At least, they knew no cowardice.
They shall not be unwept.

I sing of Marshall, Field, and Chase;
Of Roger Taney's famous case;
Of Blair, in flowing wig and lace,
Administering law!
They had a single high ideal.
To passion they did not appeal.
Had you requested a "new deal,"
They might have answered "Faugh!"

I sing of Livingston and Swayne;
Of Barbour, Daniel, Cushing, Wayne;
Of Catron, Bradley, and McLean
Who dignified the Court.
It seems superfluous to state
That if they chose to castigate
Each other, they confined debate
To personal retort.

These gentlemen of other days
Were not imbued with modern ways.
Their judgments to the world's amaze,
In fairness were ingrained.
A Todd would not have known a Black;
Ward Hunt would loathe Frankfurter's claque;
John Jay had manners and their lack
In Jackson would have pained.

One doubts that Gabriel Duval—
To judge from portraits on the wall—
For Roberts' eloquence would fall,
Or that of Stanley Reed;
One scarcely pictures old Lamar
(Lucius Q. C.) going so far
As offering Murphy a cigar
After a social "feed";

Nor Charleston's Rutledge getting gay
With Rutledge out of Ioway—
Not that I mean in any way
To criticize our boys!
It's simply that their politics
With ancient notions do not mix—
A jest with Holmes across the Styx
Undoubtedly enjoys!

THE OPA MOURNER

He shuffled sadly to the bar
And gave a kind of screech.
"I'll have," he sobbed, "some caviar
"And Pepper's maiden speech."

The barman wiped a whiskey glass,
As lazy as a sloth.
His voice was callous, crude and crass:
"Oh, yeah? We're out of both."

"Then how about," the stranger cried,
"Some paper like PM?"
The barman, clear and quick, replied:
"I used it – well, ahem!"

"Then give me," sighed the woeful wreck,
"Earl Browder's latest dope,
"And mix it with a horse's neck
"So I'll get drunk – I hope."

"My friend," said I, in tones of silk,
"Those drinks are poisoned stuff.
"Would not be a double malted milk
"And Dixon be enough?

"Or do you mourn some lovely gal
"With eyes like precious stones?
"Perhaps your uncle died, old pal,
"And you've mislaid his bones?

"Your wife, perchance, has shot herself?
"Your dog has lost a pup?
"So what? There's more upon the shelf.
"Cheer up, old bean! Cheer up!"

He turned on me the sullen eyes
Of a caged catamount.
He growled: "I mourn no girl's demise.
"I grieve for things that count.

"I weep the New Deal alphabet
"Now falling to decay,
"From NRA, the teachers pet,
"To now—the OPA!"

My heart began to skip and jump.
I felt my spirits sink.
I gave the bar a mighty thump:
"Bartender, fix a drink!"

A PMF the barman served,
With comprehending grin—
The PMF he well deserved—
The Potent Mickey Finn!

Our Modern Oracles

I wish I were an Oracle
Upon a Delphic shelf,
Just peering out with lusty shout
To boast about myself.
It must be fine to so divine
The future of the race
That one can grab a microphone
And blab it every place,
Interpreting each passing phase
Of politics and war,
And telling people how to vote
And what they're voting for;
Warning the nation of its fate
With sibylline aplomb
While urging that we give our foes
The deadly atom bomb!

O for the impudence of this
Oracular technique
Which bring our prophets profits, too—
One thousand bucks a week!
If I possessed the bigot's zest—
That old Chautauqua snap—
My eloquence on world events
Would quickly change the map.
I'd study first some "liberal" seer
Whose strategy had clicked,
So I might mold the moron mind
By yelling "I predict"......
The fact that world events did not
Turn out as I'd reveal
Would not, I find, in any way
Discredit my appeal.
Indeed, the less my horoscopes

And omens were fulfilled,
The more my inspired auguries
With printed facts I'd gild.

I'd take each INS dispatch,
Each AP, UP wire—
Into my listeners' eager ears
Their contents I would fire:
"Friends, I predict that Truman's views
Will make the Arabs sore...
(I read it in the daily news)...
I predict, furthermore,
That Russia will a half a million Austrians deport...
(I glimpsed it just this second in
A Viennese report)...
And I predict the British loan—
This is no idle guess—
Will pass the House by 5 to 1...
(According to the press)"...
Thus, bellowing in Winchellese,
Would I prognosticate
A remedy for each disease
Disordering the state;
Nor would my conscience (had I one)
Emit a mournful cry
Because it knew each ill was due
To persons such as I.

But I am not an Oracle
Upon a Delphic ridge,
So I shall smile and wait awhile
(Although I don't play bridge),
And see if, as our Oracles
So confidently shout,
The old ideas of right and wrong
Are really inside out;
And if the side I represent

Is permanently licked
By an illiberal liberal gent
Whinnying "I predict".....
For I don't dare—an amateur—
To gaze in crystal globes
And prophecy who next July
Will wear Fred Vinson's robes;
Or, save for casual ideas,
Attempt to tell the world
By whom and what at just which spot
Whose flag will be unfurled.
I do not know if Borneo
Will British be or Dutch;
If Black or Jackson will resign –
It doesn't matter much!
I won't forecast if OPA
The Senate will revive,
But I predict the USA,
Despite all, will survive;
And I predict that one bright day,
Surfeited by their bunk,
Listeners will take their Oracles
And toss them out for junk!

THE KAVALIER'S KRY

(With apologies—humble ones—to Longfellow)

Listen, ye kleagles, and ye shall hear
Of the gallant kry of a kavalier,
Anyone who knows politics
Will remember that famous day and year.

He said to his friend: "If the Ku Klux march
In a klavalcade to Atlanta tonight,
Hang a klavern aloft in the belfry arch
Of the cyclop's lodge as a signal light—
One if by land and two if by sea,
And I in a near-by klub shall be
Ready to ride and spread the alarm
To keep our kountrymen safe from harm,
And kall our komrades to up and to arm."

Then he said "Koo-koo!" and with muffled shriek
Silently rowed down the Chesapeake,
Just as the moon rose over the bay
Where a gruesome fleet of pleasure kraft lay
Like phantom ships—each sail like a gown
Worn as a kloak by some hooded klown,
and huge black hulks that were magnified
By the kavalier's terrors in the tide.

Meanwhile his friend through kurious places
Wanders and watches with eager eyes,
Till in the silence around him be spies
(Or thinks that he does) a klonvokation
Dressed in sheet and klean, krisp pillowcases—
A ghostly konklave of ghastly size
Threatening the safety of the nation!

Then he klimbed the tower of the cyclop's lodge,
Up the krumbling stairs with krafty tread

To the belfry chamber overhead—
And startled the klansmen who ran hodge-podge,
Klattering from korners that round him made
Masses and moving shapes of shade.

Meanwhile, protected on every side
By sturdy policemen—Atlanta's pride—
on Georgia's soil walked the kavalier.
Now he patted his lawyer's hand,
Now, nervously, took a noble stand;
Then, impetuous, sniffed and smelt,
And turned and tightened his slipping belt;
But mostly he kwivvered, ready to dodge
Any shot that might come from the cyclop's lodge
As it rose above the graves on the hill,
Lonely and spectral and somber and still.
And lo! as he looks, on the belfry's height
A klimmer and then a kleam of light!
He springs in the air; through the microphone
Arises his high-pitched, kwavering tone—
Till a Kleagle flees with a long sad moan!

A hurry of hoofs in Atlanta's street,
A kluck in the moonlight, a klonk in the dark,
And beneath, from the pavement, in passing, a spark
Struck out by a running klansman's feet:
That was all! And yet, through the gloom and the light,
The fate of a nation was balanced that night;
And the spark struck out by that klansman in flight
Kindles the land into flame with its heat!

So through the night talked the kavalier:
And so through the night went his kry of alarm
To keep all his kountrymen safe from harm—
A cry of defiance and not of fear,
A voice in the darkness, a knock at the door,
And a word that shall echo forevermore!

For—let grand dragons say what they may,
And despite the skreams of the KKK—
In the hour of darkness and peril and kneed
The people will waken and listen to hear
Those klannish hoofbeats (Kids, take heed!)
And the gallant kry of the kavalier!

THE SOCIAL SEASONS OF WASHINGTON

Politics, scandal, tourists and fleas,
Pink cherry blossoms, afternoon teas,
Cocktails and oysters, primrose and daisy,
Senator So-and-so talking like crazy,
Artists that day dream, alarm clocks that ring—
This, friend, is Washington in the spring!

Politics, scandal, hustle and heat,
Pink, angry faces; no one to meet;
Cocktails sans oysters, days that are lazy,
Senator So-and-so talking like crazy.
Feuds with the house-maid, chats with the plumber—
This, bo, is Washington in the summer!

Politics, scandal, wind gusts and clouds,
Pink, falling oak leaves; omens like shrouds;
Cocktails and oysters, days that are hazy,
Senator So-and-so campaigning like crazy,
People that matter, people that call—
This, pal, is Washington in the fall!

Politics, scandal, colds in the head,
Pinks in the parlor talking deep "red",
Cocktails and oysters, nights that are hazy,
Senator So-and-so back—and he's crazy!
Bridge fiends that squabble, ice cubes that splinter—
This, sir, is Washington in the winter!

Farewell to the Seventy-Ninth Congress

(with certain exceptions)

FAREWELL, great legislators! Are you through at last
With your inspired and Herculean job?
O the rich memory of those bills you passed!
O how your record makes one's heart to throb!

Ah, wonder men! Since you must say "Adieu,"
Accept the tribute an admirer begs
On your departure to present to you—
This nice, dead tomcat and these rotten eggs!

What opportunity was yours, ye dopes!
What fine, unrivaled chance to garner fame!
Pray, have you seized it, sirs, and raised fair hopes!
Or does your generation mutter "Shame!"?

Your consciences shall tell the truth—not I.
Votes, too, perchance—although the people's will
Sometimes seems weak if represented by
Those oafs it sends to climb the magic hill!

So let us scatter, gents—or should I say
"Statesmen"? I fear you are not on the beam
Sufficiently to get the satire. Nay,
How can one joke on such a tragic theme?

In parting, just a word: if bitter chaff
Heralds the leaving of the men we hailed,
Will you not use it as an epitaph:
"HE HAD A NOBLE TASK TO DO—AND FAILED!"

GUS GLOOBAR'S FATE

(Inspired by a visit to the Washington Zoo)

The keeper of a first-rate zoo
Must be possessed of social tact.
He bows discreetly to the gnu,
And shows the monkeys how to act.
He asks the elephant's advice
On elephantine etiquette.
He keeps a touch of something nice
In knitted patterns for each pet.
Perhaps—when all the beasts are fed
And it is getting sort of late—
He'll tell you, 'ere he goes to bed,
Of poor Gus Gloobar's dreadful fate!

Gus couldn't learn to run a zoo.
His tactics turned the camel gray.
He simply ruined the kangaroo.
He made the walrus declasse.
He never once removed his hat
When speaking to the lion cubs.
He called the haughty tapir "Pat."
He stopped the rhino's beauty rubs.
One day he placed the low baboon
Beside the high-brow zebra colt;
The zebra went into a swoon
And all the zoo went in revolt!

In berserk rage the porcupine
Attacked Gus with a poisoned quill.
The wild hyena gave a whine,
And crushed him like a dollar bill.
The grizzly bear broke through the fray
And battered him with furry paws,
Declaring Gus in every way

Had violated nature's laws.
The tiger who, with fret and fuss,
Had pleaded for a manicure,
Tore off his stripes and sprang at Gus,
Exclaiming: "This I'll not endure!"

They buried Gus (or what remained)
And very soon the zoo grew calm.
The docile animals refrained
From causing any more alarm.
The city fathers duly sent
A proper keeper for the job.
He is so kind and competent
He makes the virgin llamas sob.
The wolf salutes him with a leer;
The elephant with lifted trunk
The only one who won't revere
Their charming keeper is a skunk!

FIRST HORSEBACK RIDE SINCE '41

It isn't the oily touch of the reins;
It isn't the rub of the saddle;
It isn't the blisters, the cramps or the pains
Induced by the creature you straddle.
The sneers of a steed and the snorts of a friend
Are nothing at which one should boggle,
But, frankly, the thing I resent in the end
Is this joggety-jiggety-joggle!

O gallops and canters are pleasure intense
As we fly over hedges and boulders!
(I'll skip that bad spill when I fell at the fence,
And the consequent wrench in my shoulders),
But—let grooms and cowboys slyly deride!
Let stablemen snigger and giggle!—
I cannot abide in the nag I bestride
This jiggety-joggety-jiggle!

They tell me horseman who's fond of his mount
Deliberately trots as he snoozes.
And that a real horse who's of any account
Can trot without giving you bruises—
But I am a rider without any pride
At whom all the hunting set goggle.
And I WILL not ride, with my breakfast inside,
At a joggety-jiggety-joggle!

LA FIESTA Y LA SIESTA

The fiesta and siesta one can easily confuse.
The siesta, as you've guessed, sir, is your post-fiesta snooze;
Thus, fiesta is a test to one's capacity for rhumba,
While siesta is a rest to well digest a fruta bomba.

On a "dia de fiesta" all the church bells gaily ring;
All the peons eat bananas; all the big rancheros sing;
All the shutters wide are opened to admit the glare and heat,
Lest a thought of a siesta dare to pester those who eat.

But on "dias de siesta"—that's to say, the other six—
All the peons and rancheros play at party politics;
While, behind the battened shutters, you can hear the snores resound
And it's "viva la siesta" until Sunday rolls around.

Summer is ending. The days grow shorter, cocktail hours longer, blankets thicker. There is a chill in the air. All eyes turn homeward. Goodby, then, to Newport and its stuffy dowagers! Goodby to New Mexico and its golden sunsets! Goodby to the Southampton mouse races! Goodby to Bar Harbor with its tennis and drinking! Goodby to Arizona and its Painted Desert and to Hollywood and its painted faces!

Goodby, America! I am going back to Washington!

Goodby to incredible dinners that are scheduled for 8 o'clock—and surprisingly, start at that hour! Goodby to fat Texas steers moodily chewing the cud and to fat Indians moodily selling turquoise rings! Goodby to ministers who are somehow connected with churches and to expansive, shifty-eyed individuals who are gushingly presented as "Ambassadors of Good Will!" Goodby to night clubs labeled "exclusive," catering to hundreds of diners and selling three roses as a boutonniere for $4.50! Goodby to Carl Van Vechten intelligentsia suppers where guests are formally introduced to the servants before sitting down to table!

Goodby to gooey weddings where the bridesmaids wear trailing dresses of pink marquisette and Pink Lady cocktails are served against a background of shell pink roses! Goodby to houses so grandiose that the French chef lives in an atmosphere of feudal magnificence! Goodby to fabulous gatherings where seldom is heard a discouraging word—or an intelligent word, either! Goodby to roulette tables where each blue chip represents $1,000, where players appear in shirtsleeves and where only the croupier wears a bow tie! Goodby to bars so long that the man drinking whisky at the far end is actually in the next block! Goodby to speedboats that bounce blithely over the blue waves and to horses that bounce blithely over the blue grass! Goodby to great open faces that beam at mention of Henry Wallace (the dopes) and are clouded only by the first faint shadows of doubt!

Goodby, America! I am going home!

I am going to a strange city where people are invited to an 8 o'clock dinner which begins at 9; where you are tacitly supposed not to arrive on time and would enrage your host if you did! I am going to a city where the only steers are those given by lobbyists or the nephew of a Senator: where Indians live in a rented mansion filled with ancestral portraits, serve excellent dry Martinis and wear turbans; where ministers and ambassadors are more concerned with political pull and social prestige than with churches and good will, and where night clubs are never labeled exclusive and seldom are—although One-Eyed Connelly is reputed to have been admitted to one after flourishing a baseball pass signed by Happy Chandler!

Goodby, America! I am going home!

I am going to a city where the intelligentsia are divided between the rich and the poor; the rich, who eat little suppers by candlelight in quaint Georgetown homes, discuss the liberal trend and get very drunk (in either case their servants would decline to be introduced to them). I am going to a city where Russian Communists dwell elegantly in a marble palace and have huge stores of black caviar and vodka for the special delectation of American bourgeois and capitalists; where "pink" is a term used more often in a political group than at a fashionable wedding; where at least one chef lives in feudal magnificence in the home of a man who keeps Josef Stalin's autographed photo on his dresser, and where the most important house in town is painted a severe white and is dignified in appearance without being in any way grandiose!

Goodby, America! I am going home!

I am going to a city where roulette tables are raided by police; where there are plenty of stuffed shirts but lamentably few shirtsleeves and where the Attorney General is noted more for his bow ties than for his handling of the Justice Department which is adequately run by the "boys in the basement." I am going to a city where the shortest bars are the smartest and where you have to sit down at a table, anyway, before they will serve you a drink; where you can't buy whisky legally on Sunday and yet it's considered an insult to offer a guest a glass of sherry. I am going to a city where Speed is the name of a London distiller whose associate is named Saccone; where "horses" is only a part of a phrase and where Wallace is a way of life. I am going to a city where fish spears are oyster forks, friends are the persons you met yesterday, Faith is an Irish expression, Hope is a comedian and Charity an embassy crush where you buy rag dolls for $6 each.

Goodby, America! I am going to your spiritual home!

WALLACE AND THE KREMLIN KID

(Parody on "The Walrus and the Carpenter" by LEWIS CARROLL)

Our diplomats were talking peace;
Talking with all their might:
They did their very best to make
The future smooth and bright—
And this was odd, because, you know,
There was no peace in sight.

Jim Byrnes was acting sulkily
Because he thought Stalin
Had got no business to be tough
After the votes were in.
"It's very rude," he said, "to have
The Kremlin butting in."

The Liberals and the Communists
Were walking close at hand:
They wept like anything to see
Such lots of foreign land.
"If this were only Russianized,"
They said, "it would be grand."

"If seven hosts of peaceful Reds
Swept it with fire and sword,
Do you suppose," Hen Wallace said,
"Culture could be restored?"
"We doubt it," said his fellow pinks,
And looked a trifle bored.

"O nations, come and walk with us!"
Hen Wallace did beseech.
"A pleasant walk, a pleasant talk
About what Liberals preach.
I hope you'll tune your radios
To hear my New York speech!"

President Truman looked at him,
But never a word he said:
And President Truman winked his eye
And shook his weary head—
Meaning to say he did not choose
To sleep in Henry's bed.

But several Liberals hurried up,
To paraphrase and quote:
Their shoes were brushed, their faces washed;
Great interest to denote—
And this was odd, because, you know,
They hadn't any vote.

Then other pinkos followed them,
At very least a score:
And thick and fast they came at last,
And more and more and more,
All asking for the Party Line,
While scrambling to the shore.

"The time has come," Hen Wallace said,
"To talk of pretty games,
Like politics and Moscow tricks—
And Russia's eastern claims—
And why a guy should hit a guy
Because he calls him names."

"But wait a bit," the Liberals cried,
"Before we have our chat;
For some of us are still in jail
And most of us are flat!"
"No hurry!" said the Kremlin Kid.
They thanked him much for that.

"A touch of red," Hen Wallace said,
"Is what we chiefly need:
A venal press and some duress
Are very good indeed—

Now if you're ready, Liberals dear,
The meeting can proceed."

"But don't shoot US!" the liberals cried,
Turning a little blue.
"After our Roosevelt record, that
Would not be fair of you!"
"The Kremlin cells," Hen Wallace said,
"Command a famous view!"

"It was so kind of you to come,
And you are very nice."
The Kremlin Kid said nothing but
"Cut us another slice!
We'd like the Western Hemisphere:
Don't make us ask you twice!"

"It seems a shame," Hen Wallace mused,
"To play them such a trick,
After we've brought them out so far
And made them feel so slick!"
The Kremlin Kid said nothing but
"The sugar's spread too thick!"

"I weep for you," Hen Wallace said:
"I deeply sympathize,"
With sobs and tears he weeded out
Those he could subsidize,
Holding a New Republic ode
Before his streaming eyes.

"O Liberals," said the Kremlin Kid,
"You've had a pleasant call!
Shall we be trotting home again?"
No answer came at all—
And this was scarcely odd, because
They'd liquidated all!

ODE TO A STEAK

Thou rare and succulent fancy of my youth!
Thou luscious memory of a vanished time,
Whose savoriness once charmed the dullest tooth;
Whose juice more sweetly flowed than any rhyme!
In what strange Arcady dost thou content
The savage appetite? Where dost thou sport
Thy alien flavor, thy remote bouquet?
Who can confirm each vague, obscure report
Regarding thee? What boots an argument?
Who knows thy fate? Who—knowing—dares to say?

Some claim that slavering tongues in Oklahoma
A deeper red from gorging Sirloin grow;
Some, that Miss Filet Mignon's rich aroma
Plays Juliet to Black Mart Romeo!
Still darker rumors hint of laden ships
That sail by night more slyly than a thief;
Of Slavic banquets where the belch uncouth
Proclaims repletion after wine and beef,
As Tito smacks his thick, responsive lips!
Who knows thy end? Who—knowing—tells the truth?

Ah, distant T-Bone! One can but surmise
Beneath whose knife and where thou dost recline;
Whose lustful greed is whetted by thy size.
It is not mine, Old Friend! It is not mine!
It is not now for us, whose cattle shake
Their horns like battle flags from coast to coast,
To please our palates! Lo!—Some prying eye
Might sue for favor with his Russian host,
Observing that Americans eat steak!
To this we've sunk, Old Pal, Yea—Thou and I!

Apology to Comrade Novikov

"The State Department said today it 'deeply regrets' any discourtesy shown to Russian Ambassador Nikolai Novikov by U.S. Customs officials in New York, but added that an investigation showed no evidence of intentional discourtesy or breach of diplomatic etiquette."
United Press, Oct. 15 1946.

O Shades of Boris Godunov!
What's this affront to Novikov?
You say our customs made him wait!
HIM! Novikov! The delegate
And the supreme ambassador
And envoy of U.S.S.R.!
HIM! Kept him waiting? O not that!
HIM! Russia's premier diplomat!
O Horrors! Can such things exist?
As well cut Stalin off our list
As snub the friends we dearly love
Like darling Mr. Novikov!

An outrage! Call Dean Acheson!
Here, Woodward...Put your white spats on
And trot up there and give them hell!
Be sure to bawl them out and tell
The customs to investigate
This insult to a sovereign state.
A phone call, sir, is not enough
When people are so crude and gruff.
Why, protocol is threatened if
These customs persons act so stiff.
Go give those dopes a nasty shovel
They can't do this to Novikov!

It's true the Russians every day
And everywhere and every way
Deride us by their attitude—
Exacting, sneering, tough and rude;
And Molotov keeps shouting "No!"
Though we implore him "Say not so";
And Pravda mocks our way of life,
While Stalin slyly whets his knife!
Still, we're all out for etiquette.
Tush, Excellency! Don't you fret...
Whatever you are thinking of,
My dear, dear Mr. Novikov!

PEACE TO MAHMUD ON HIS GOLDEN THRONE

(After gazing in awe at the glittering Turkish Embassy buffet.)

The Ottoman Empire, rich with pride,
Scattered its opulence far and wide,
And many a slave paid abject court
To the government known as the Sublime Porte.

Now that Sultan and slave are gone
The ancient tradition lingers on
As guests, enslaved by this bounty, chime:
"O Turkey triumphant! Port sublime!"

THIS STRANGE POLITENESS

(After a super-cordial greeting from a Senator who will be defeated)

Why all this new political politeness?
Why this warm handclasp and this open door,
While you, turned hypocritical, delight less
In harsh rebuff and snub than here to fore?

Don't tell me that the threat of bleak November
Has torn your ancient surliness apart
And fanned into this richly glowing ember
The kindness of your democratic heart?

A smirk supplants the snicker of the war day;
A gracious bow, the cold and casual nod;
A "See you soon" and beaming "Going your way?"
Those erstwhile frigid audiences with God!

So now you offer me a swig of whisky,
(Tut, tut, old man—forget that lousy gin!)
And—now that getting nylons isn't risky—
Why, here's a pair—and how has Mother been?

Mother is well! And you can take your liquor
And kisses, stockings, compliments and guff
And hell, Election Day will tell you quicker!
The simple truth is, pal, we've had enough.

THE OLD FAMILIAR FACES—UGH!

Be patient, friend! You have seen the end
Of many men smug and puffy;
Dave Walsh says "adieu!" Will Rogers is through,
And look what happened to Guffey!

And Mead and May are out of the way;
Marcantonio's a social leper.
Who knows? Some day you may look 'round and say:
"Hey, where's that fellow, 'Red' Pepper?"

UNTITLED [MR. & MRS. CATERPILLAR]

Clad in a coat of gorgeous green,
    Snug in her urban villa.
Reading a spiel by Betty Beale,
    Sat Mrs. Caterpillar.

Beside her, smoking his cigar,
    Relaxing with a thriller
And blowing rings or purple smoke,
    Sat Mr. Caterpillar.

"It says the winter will be cold—
    A real old-fashioned killer.
My dear, I'll need another coat,"
    Said Mrs. Caterpillar.

"I said I'll need a thicker coat."
    Her voice grew much shriller.
"I'd like to kill that Betty Beale."
    Said Mr. Caterpillar.

THE RUSSIAN SOVIET RECEPTION

"Please have a plate of Russian beef! Some vodka? Hold it—so!
Gavareesh lee-vwee po-russky? Nyet? You don't spik Russian? No?
More vodka? Da! Nice party, huh? We do it bourgeois way—
Champagne and lobster—special cards—a worker's holiday!
See! Here, a white iced Kremlin rears, with huge red star above...
And there, with polished glasses, stands the polished Novikov!
(Forget his leetle trouble with your customs men, for that
Can occasionally happen with the proletariat!)
Now here, observe the salons with their gilded, scarlet tints...
And here, the whisky-sodas and the luscious peppermints!

No better even under Tsar! We have the brains and gold
To show what our new Paradise—for worthy one—can hold.
The people? Da! But naturally you got to pick and choose.
Some tramps you got to keep outside; some beasts you must refuse.
You got to make distinctions, da? You can't have tory scum
Or fascist dogs or chauvinists—besides, they wouldn't come!
Da! Look—we got the cream! Just note who's coming up the stair—
Attorney General Clark!...Hi, Tom!...Joe Davies, I declare!
Joe wouldn't miss a time like this—he's never missed one yet...
One capitalist on Stalin's list who loves the Soviet!

Why, there's Joe Baldwin (lots of Joes!). He suffered bad defeat
Election Day. There's Guggenheim—he never can be beat!
And lo!, our pal Dean Acheson, so tall and blond and 'pink'...
(Good thing Pat Hurley lost the race—or he'd be out, I think!)
Da! Da! More vodka? Try the fish! It's Volga sturgeon, friend—
Please, won't you eat this Marxist treat? Here's some I recommend...
Lord Inverchapel?...Over there, beside the potted palms...
But don't we loathe the English? Da! But why should we have qualms?
It's just a diplomatic game where cunning counts for much...
(Oh, how I laugh to see the wily British cheat the Dutch!)
We entertain with suckling pigs and orchids in New York...
Why not push ideology with flowers and with pork?...
Shh! Quiet, friend! Please—not so loud! Sit on this davenport!

That guarded room's where Molotov is holding secret court...

Nyet! Nyet! No! No! you CAN'T go in! Dear friend, please be discreet!

That special, private, privileged room is but for the elite.

Class system? Bah! We just have rules. Some get more caviar,

More epaulettes, more rubles, drinks—perhaps a better car,

A finer house, security—while over all, the State—

Supreme—like Stalin or the Tsar—rules subjects small and great.

But, come, forgive me all this talk! Some sweet white wine perhaps?

That Leftist journalist looks drunk. That girl in silver wraps—

Is she Max Gardner's wife? Too young. Red Pepper's wife? Too slim...

There's Thomas of the CIO...I must play up to HIM...

Ah, the Patriarch of Moscow with his flowing, noble beard!...

Who dares to say religion in our country's not revered?...

Here come the Batts...Da! Da! My friend and Hendersons—here's four,

But the Leons—not the Loys—pass the guarded secret door!

You're leaving, friend?... One final cup?...Nyet?... None? You're off to bed?...

I, too!... Good night...Da! Da!... AND NOW TO WRITE DOWN WHAT HE
    SAID!"

The Christmas rush was over and—relaxing by the fire—
Old Santa Claus kicked off his boots and sighed: "I must retire...
"It used to be a lot of fun in 1884,
"But now, delivering presents has become a dreadful chore."
He sighed again and thoughtfully refilled his meerschaum pipe,
Recalling yuletide memories when love and youth were ripe.
His favorite reindeer, Blitzen, came and nuzzled at his hand.
"Yes, Blitzen," said his master, "that old Washington was grand.
"Remember Dupont Circle with its mansions all around,
"Before they built the tunnel and we all went underground?
"The ugly British Embassy with crown above the gate,
"Instead of what they have today—all glass and gleaming plate?
"The Edson Bradley castle with its chapel and its hall
"Where dowagers with gold lorgnettes admired the Christmas ball?
"No speed cops chased the fleeing car that raced out Northeast way—
"Who ever knew a hansom cab do thirteen miles a day?
"That was the time when Senators wore lovely stovepipe hats
"And lived around the Capitol in inexpensive flats.
"A quiet game of poker they considered a carouse
"And thought that only idiots would rent a Georgetown house.
"That was the time when Santa Claus meant more than Christmas yells.
"And phonies shuffling through the stores and ringing little bells,
"And traffic stalled for countless blocks, and dopes with aching feet
"Screaming for taxis, packed like rats along a swarming street.
"And singers singing carols to extol some Polish king,
"King Wencelus would certainly have hanged them in a ring!
"I like to think of Christmas when the gift from Cousin Kate
"Was a knitted woolen muffler—not a pack of real estate.
"When people swept their chimneys out and hung the family stocking...
"Ah, that was Christmas, Blitzen! But today it's really shocking!"
Old Santa paused to ruminate and glance about his shelves
And shout "Look out! Don't break it! at his hustling, bustling elves.
"Then, puffing at his pipe once more, he cleared his throat and said:
"Yes, yes, the Washington I used to know is dead.

"It's deader than a Christmas lush: it's vanished like the Dodo.

"Today I carry burdens that would kill a Quasimodo.

"It was nice to bring the toys in those splendid, sparkling times—

"The shawls and fans, the good cigars, the music box with chimes

"That played old fashioned waltzes, the tasseled boudoir lamp,

"The shaving mug stamped "Henry" with a very fancy stamp.

"The cameos, the brooches and the charming topaz rings.

"The donkey cart, the china doll—all kinds of lovely things.

"Under Cleveland and McKinley it was tabby cats and sherry,

"And—if the minister approved—a case of Tom & Jerry.

"Then later came the Teddy bears and even Taft o'possums—

"I remember under Wilson it was canes and orange blossoms.

"Today the choosey items on my modern Christmas list

"Are vodka jugs and books that teach my reindeer how to Twist!

"Big snazzy planes, electric trains (I used to like the kind

You wound up with a simple key. You see I'm far behind).

 "Cosmetic gadgets shooting scent from an exotic gun

"Dueling pistols (fake of course) marked 1761.

"Ashtrays that never hold their own, plastic torpedo boats—

"That sink at sight of a waveless sea—only the rudder floats.

"Velvet zebras with jeweled eyes, porcelain objets d'art.

"Everything that you'll never need to stock your portable bar.

"This and that and the other junk you couldn't cherish less—

"A sable trunk, an Aztec vase, a Persian motif dress,...

"Is it for this I fill our sleigh and hurry over the roofs?

"Is it for this I slave and sweat and polish your dainty hoofs!"

Old Santa's shout rang loudly out. The elves all turned to stare.

While Blitzen's fur rose stiffly up—each individual hair.

Then, tapping out the ashes from his now extinguished pipe.

The good saint gave his faithful friend a sharp resounding swipe.

His voice rose to a kind of shriek. "Yes, Blitzen, this is it!"

One of the elves dropped a crystal star and another elf threw a fit.

"I ask you, Blitzen, man to beast, what are we going to do?

"If this is the way it is today, what about '62?"

MUSINGS

(Inspired by the unveiling of La Gioconda at the National Gallery)

Draw up your chairs! Come closer, friends! Relax and rest awhile
And hearken to the story of the Mona Lisa smile!
The story runs—or so we've heard—that on a certain night
Twelve hundred persons sought to view a rare and wondrous sight:
The fabled Mona Lisa, who had come from overseas
To bring a little culture to our aborigines.
Before the doors were opened to admit the cultured mob,
All the cultured cops stood ready—every "flic" was on the job.
There was cultured "boeuf" at dinner in the Embassy of France;
There was culture in the way that Angie Duke had pressed his pants
(There undoubtedly was culture, too, in Angie's spot remover);
And culture in the FBI of Monsieur Edgar Hoover.

The President arrived to make a "glad-to-have-you" speech.
As past they filed, the crowd went wild and tried his side to reach.
The elevators failed to work, the microphone "aussi,"
So Malraux's words were never heard on Vinci, called "Vansee"!
Like waves that beat on rugged shores, great clamoring arose
As people whanged and clanged and banged and trod on others' toes.
Then lo! while vast confusion reigned, a kind of rosy glow
Suffused the Mona Lisa's face and—critics tell us so—
Her mouth relaxed, her lips turned up, and those Italian teeth
Unclenched and (well we would have blenched!) revealed "le gorge" beneath.
And loud the Mona Lisa laughed; her mirth did ring throughout—
You really couldn't blame her: she had lots to laugh about!

THE UNSEEN VISITOR

'Twas the night before Christmas and throughout D.C.
'Twas what you'd expect such a night to be—
Calm as a typhoon, dull as a scene
By the great Picasso or a book by Celine...
Silent as magpies...houses aglow
With candles and holly and mistletoe...
Children all laughing...pre-Christmas cheer
On Wisconsin avenue (pretzels and beer)
Bored politicians talked politics
In a downtown club until ten past six.
At half past seven a bright little lad
Went out and bought the wrong tie for his Dad.
At half-past eight, with the Christmas tree done,
His Dad bought the wrong kind of sled for his son.

At nine a white-whiskered gent won applause
By playing the lead role of Santa Claus.
Christmas carolers roamed by the scores,
Pounding the knockers on Georgetown doors
To disturb citizens spending their time
Watching a TV thriller on crime.
By eleven-forty or thereabout
Some lights and all cats were quickly put out.
At midnight, music from the churches pealed,
The cold grew intense. Car engines congealed.
A protocol expert leaned back and sighed,
Taking his final limousine ride
Through Rock Creek Park, enjoying the view;
The economy drive gets his chauffeur, too.

About one o'clock a long, black cloud
Enveloped the moon. It hung like a shroud.
Three minutes later some drunk gave a shout
And pointed skyward—the moon had come out.
Pale stars quivered, remote in the sky.

A child in its crib started to cry,
"I want Santa Claus." Strange to relate,
Santa Claus heard her—even that late.
Around two-thirty a creaky sleigh
Jolted and sloshed down the Milky Way.
Known to the world but seen by none,
Its reindeer headed for Washington.
A fat, jolly fellow with cute pink ears
Had driven this sleigh for a thousand years.
He steered his reindeer with deft, sure hand
'Mid constellations sparkling and grand.
Venus and Neptune and Little Bear
Turned on the old man their brilliant stare.
Orion threw him a dazzling look
And blazing Sirus sizzled and shook.
But beams and sunbursts each fiery mile
Could add no radiance to Santa's smile.

The clocks struck three. High above the town
Santa Claus' reindeer came zooming down.
Washington slept as the great sleigh bobbed
(Except for a gas station being robbed!)
Washington slept in its special way.
Some lay worrying about Christmas bills;
Some had nightmares; others had chills
At the very idea of missing a bet
By snubbing the new White House social set.
Vegetarians who detested meat
Dreamed of deer sausage, that special treat
Of President Johnson's and—when they awoke—
Decided to buy some, even though they'd choke.

Senators slept under crazy quilts
And dreamed that constituents perched on stilts,
Crazy constituents, peeked through the shade
And whispered "budget" and "foreign aid"
And "Navy bases" and "civil rights."

(How can Senators sleep of night?)
Congressmen, too, slept uneasy sleep,
Woke up, took sleeping pills, counted sheep,
Counted expenditures, counted votes,
Got up and shivered in overcoats.
Diplomats slept, by exhaustion drugged,
But jumped up thinking the phone was bugged.
And rushed to a table to read again
A deciphered cable from Greece or Spain.

Washington slept as the sleigh swept by—
A tinkle of bells and hooves in the sky—
A prancing, entrancingly lovely sight.
Turning and twisting high in the night,
Soaring and pouring a magic glow
On the sleeping city far below—
Unseen, yet bringing a touch of mirth.
A hint of good humor to those on earth
And faith and kindness and charity
On this Christmas of nineteen sixty-three!

THE POLITICAL LION

The Political Lion got up at eight
And yawned, and growled at his empty plate,
Then (he was never a very late sleeper)
He rang the bell and yelled for the keeper.
"So what's the matter?" the keeper said.
"I suppose you want to have breakfast in bed
"With bacon and eggs and coffee and toast,
"And read the news in the Washington Post!"

The Political Lion just looked at his claws
And answered, "Now, don't get rude, because
"I had to eat two keepers last week
"And that's not good for a lion's physique.
"I don't want coffee, I don't want toast.
"And I never read the Washington Post.
"No, what I'd like is antelope rib
"And a spot of tea and the Herald Trib."

The keeper's eyes glowed like kidney stew
As he said, "I've been at the Washington Zoo
"For only three days but I never thought
"I'd have a crime like this to report.
"We're all good Democrats here, Mr. Lion,
"The elephant's the only critter I spy on.
"Do you think you're special or sort of immune?
"The White House don't take the Herald Tribune!"

The Political Lion pulled skin from his claws.
It wasn't his skin but the keeper's because
What was left of the keeper was overtones
Of blood and gristle and hair and bones.
When they'd swept it up and carried out most
Of the mess wrapped up in the Washington Post.
The lion said: "Gentlemen, my delight
"Is to read whatever good writers write.

"They may damn lions. They may be rough,
"But a lion in politics takes that stuff.
"Right now I'm hungry—and that's no fib!—
"So how about food and the Herald Trib?"

ACKNOWLEDGEMENTS

There are so many people to thank for this book that it is difficult for me to claim that I did anything.

First there is Diana Keesee and her parents Joseph and Eileen Kingsbury-Smith.

My father and the Kingsbury-Smiths met in Paris where Joe was head of International News Service. Later Joe moved to New York to head the merger of UP and INS where the friendship continued.

I received a call in the summer of 2016 asking if I was the son of George Abell. Diana Keesee, the daughter of the Kingsbury-Smiths, told me she had poems of my father which she had found when she sifted through her parents' papers. I drove to her home in Middleburg, VA and was delighted to find four file folders, each with a pile of poems. Most had been typed with an Olivetti, a machine I remembered my father used. Some had changes made in my father's handwriting. Many I remembered having seen before. Altogether, there were 125 pieces of verse; some appeared in two folders. Why, why, why?

We'll never know, but I am very grateful to Diana and her parents.

My son, Dan Tyler Abell, saved several poems including one written on the occasion of his birth in 1958, which his mother Bess put in his baby book.

My friend Don Lindberg self-published two books of photography and encouraged me to dig in. Joe Arnold, my nephew, had published a book of his paintings and used that experience to guide me.

My friend and favorite neighbor, Frank Chechile, undertook to do the proofreading which is perhaps the world's most tiresome task. A thousand thanks to Frank.

Neal Gillen, a fellow lawyer, has written and self-published eleven books and counting. He was very accommodating with his advice, as was Chris Poch.

Darlene Swanson did the cover design and layout. Tom Berger did even more proofreading.

I've saved the best for last. Christy Thrailkill typed all of the poems, took pictures, interacted with printers, editors, and steered the course to its final conclusion. Which is where you the reader picked it up, and I therefore acknowledge that you the reader are the most important element in the book. Without you this never would have been done.

Thank you all.

Tyler Abell

INDEX

Made in the USA
Middletown, DE
08 September 2019